The Act of "88"

By: Darla Mae Dudley

Library of Congress Control Number:
2015916443

CreateSpace Independent
Publishing Platform,
North Charleston, SC

1

Chapter 1

It was 1988 and the campaign promises that landed the young Midwestern Senator in Office was about to make an impact on our country that would be in the history books as the most incredible event since the great depression.

In his active campaign for President, the young and ambitious Senator Kent had promised to clean up the country. He wasn't quite sure how to go about this, but his first thought was to ban dumping and issue a mandatory recycling law. So shortly after his overwhelming election, the newly elected President had one of the other

Senators draft up the proposal and under the direction of the President of the United States, sending a proposed bill through the House and Senate called the Act of '88.

It was later in the Oval Office that the newly elected President along with various staff members and members of the House and Senate were invited for a briefing. "Mr. President, how do we go about this?" Questioned by several of the Congressman, it was also on the other members thoughts as well.

"Simmer down now," as the Speaker of the House was presiding at Congress that day, and was at the pulpit, started banging his hammer to get everyone's attention; as he gives the President the microphone.

The President clears his throat and says, "Ladies and Gentlemen, I am sure that you are wondering what I have gathered you here for. I am proposing to close the landfills that have reached their maximum capacity and we are going to force the country into using other means of disposal."

A sudden outburst was heard as well as whispering among several House members. Soon the "bang, bang, bang" of the hammer at the pulpit was heard.

Again the President spoke. "I have assigned a committee to look into alternative ways of disposal." As some gentlemen in black suits hand out a rather large pamphlet to each of the members of both the House and Senate, He then continues to speak saying, "I have had extensive research done on this matter as you will read in this proposal. You will also find that there states various means of disposal as well as uses for garbage waste; such as recycling. The fact is lumber can be turned into particle board. Glass as well as paper and aluminum cans, also can be recycled.

Even tires can be shredded into chips and burned to create fuel for energy or used for landscaping and even used as a base for building roads. Everything that man makes can be turned into another source of income and this my dear friends could lower taxes!"

At that remark everyone applauded and the conversations between the House and Senate members in the meeting was bustling with both ideas and concerns. The President steps down from the podium and walks around shaking hands and having small talk with all the men and women in the room that appeared to be supportive of what he was saying for the moment.

Later that evening the President sat down with his wife to discuss the days' activities. "Darling" she said, "This garbage thing, do you really think it will work?"

He replies, "My dear I think if I don't try, the country is going to have a serious problem. I have looked into this myself as well as talked with several people.

You remember the luncheon we had with the Mayor of New York last year." She answers with a smile, "Yes I remember that well; matter of fact I still have those newspaper clipping from the garbage barge incident, let me get them for you." As she leaves the room to get the folder that she had put them in. A few minutes later she walks back into the room with a large envelope and hands it to her husband. As he pulls several clipping out of the envelope and reads the newspaper articles. "Listen to this dear," as he reads the article. "New

York Times... There has always been value in trash for those who know where to find it." Putting down the newspaper article on the table, the President looks at his wife and says, "Did you hear what that said, now a days there is also value in disposing of trash, if one can find a place to put it. (They both start laughing). "Let me read on" he says to her as the President continues, "The National Waste Corporation finds itself with an embarrassment of trash floating about the Atlantic and Gulf of Mexico on a barge. Its fate remains unclear, but serves as a warning that more such embarrassments are likely to occur in the absence of sound planning.

National Waste buys bailed business trash and sells it to others who extract and use its minerals or calories. In 1987, a loaded seagoing barge with waste from Long Island City, New York, was towed to Morehead City, North Carolina. Another company bought the trash who intended to unload it in a methane-generating waste disposal site that operates at a local dump. But local officials intervened and forbid the unloading of outside and out of state trash in their dwindling dump site. Since then the garbage has cruised the Gulf of Mexico like a cursed sailor with no place to call home". Suddenly the First Lady jumped up... as she replies, "You know dear, this resistance is as much political as economic. No elected official could face a campaign in which he stood accused of letting outsiders soil his native land with others' waste." A sudden sparkle flashes in the President's eyes as he replies to his wife's statement. "You are exactly correct...but let me read on what this article says." Getting excited he reads on. "The outcast barge still symbolizes the premium of disappearing dump space and the urgency of a better solid waste management. This can only mean that by removing useful resources from waste and incinerating at high temperatures the non-useful residues we can reduce their volume. Unknown to most the existing technology makes it possible to reduce residues to ten percent of the original volume and this amount we can manage with." The First Lady looks stunned and says, "I didn't realize that; you know unless the country gets serious about installing systems for incineration and recovery, the cruising garbage barge, beyond any doubt will only become a growing homeless fleet." (The President puts down the article) Again looking at his wife with a serious look he says to her, "This is exactly what I am talking about! This garbage problem has gone too far. We need to attend to this issue immediately. It has been on my mind since the incident occurred last year and that is why I based my campaign on the clean-up of the country. This is a very serious problem! More so then anyone could possibly imagine. If we don't resolve this on a Federal level, then ten (10) years from now it will be too late."

The First Lady gets up from her chair and stretches a bit then looks at her husband and says to him; "Well enough of this dear, it is getting late and we can talk more about this tomorrow. Good night dear, don't stay up too late." As she leaves the room, the President gets out of his chair and walks over to the bar and pours himself a glass of brandy. Coming from Kentucky his family back in the day were moonshiners. The President was rather fond of the home brew when he could sneak it in, but under the circumstances, he kept it quiet. The media would have a field day on this subject and with the religious votes that put him in office, he was smart to keep it under his hat so to speak, so he never talked about it.

As he sat back into his chair with glass in hand, he thought about the conversation that he had with his wife as he kept looking at the newspaper clippings that were on the coffee table. Thinking to himself about the days' events and the positive response that he got from Congress, he whispered to himself, "I think that we can really do something good for the country. I know that this will not be easy but in the long run this will be my legacy." Putting his glass down on the table, he gets up and walks out of the room.

Chapter 2

The next morning came quickly as did the rain. It rained the whole day so both the President and First Lady had their secretary's reschedule all appointments and cleared their calendars for one day. That afternoon standing at the window of the Oval Office the President watched the rain come down as the First Lady sat on the sofa across the room from her husband's desk as she softly speaks to him. "Are you still thinking about that garbage barge stuff dear?" The President turns to her smiling and says, "You can read my mind can't you, and by the way thank you, I am glad we took the day off.

I needed to clear my head and not have everyone's opinion on this subject today." Walking over to the sofa he sits down and pats her on her leg and continues to speak saying, "That is all I can think about right now. If you would be as so kind to have your team do research on what is going on with this barge, where it is, you know the rest. I would like to be informed of where it has been and what the plans for this thing are. Also, how do storms affect the trash that is bundled and have they lost any of the garbage piled up? You know, have the team find out the scoop on this thing. I need to know all the facts on this." The First Lady gets up turning to her husband and says, "I will have my staff quietly look into this so as not to draw any attention from your staff, after all you know how rumors fly in this town." The President gives his wife a kiss and says to her, "I knew I could depend on you to handle this delicate situation discretely." The President turns and walks toward his desk as his wife leaves the room she stops at the door to remind him that dinner will be served at seven and that the Senator from Kentucky and his wife were the invited guests for the evening. The President gets a smile on his face as the First Lady laughs, knowing what he is grinning about.

The rest of the afternoon goes quickly with very little interruptions; the President goes through the pile of paper on his desk of bill proposals and invitations jotting down notes or instructions on the yellow post-its attached to the documents for approval before handing them over to his secretarial staff to handle. Unlike most Presidents, this one decided to involve himself in the day to day activities. He told his staff that he wanted to be in the loop with what was coming and going out of his office and that nothing was to go out without at least an initial from him on the documents. Because of this request, the First Lady would take the initiative to clear his calendar at least twice a month so that her husband could get a handle on some of the paperwork that would pile up. She was his right hand and would review most of what went through his office knowing full well his stand on what he would accept and not accept. This was a team effort going to the White House. The First Lady knew her husband's strengths and weaknesses and she was always there at his side to support him on the things that she knew would be difficult or a problem. Fortunately for him, she could gracefully handle things that he could not, so politically it worked out well for the both of them.

The evening came and Senator Tom Edwards of Kentucky and his wife

Elaine were a welcome sight for the President. He and Tom went to Harvard together and had a lot of catching up to do. As always, Tom had a mason jar wrapped up in a brown paper wrapping from the home place, as the President went over to the bar to get some shot glasses for a before dinner toast.

The First Lady and Elaine were actually second cousins. Alexandria (Alex) the First Lady was Elaine's bridesmaid at her and Tom's wedding. When the President (Jim Kent) and Alex got married, Elaine reciprocated and was her maid of honor. It was nice to be able to have a meal here in the White House with actual family and not talk politics. Elaine filled in Alex with all that was going on in Kentucky as well as all the gossip of the family back home in Lexington.

Tom and the President (Jim) reminisced about the hunting and fishing trips that they took over the years, stretching the truth while drinking shots of Kentucky moonshine between the bites of dinner. Sitting at the table, eating and visiting with their friends was the ending of an unusually quiet day in Washington.

Early the next morning the President found himself again in his favorite chair pondering the events of several days before and the discussion that he and his wife had.

As the smoke from his pipe swirled upward and his fingers tapping on the arm of the large wing-backed chair; he wiggled his toe through a small hole in his sock then grinned as he looked down. Remembering with his status how improper this was. Quickly while no-one was around, he slipped on his shoes and made his way to the dining room.

Saying nothing, he started jotting down the days' activities from his calendar on a yellow legal pad, winking occasionally to his wife at the other end of the table. Morning was a time to gather thoughts; so it was a tradition never to talk during the morning meal. Even the staff was well informed of this ritual. With the exception of a soft clatter of a cup and saucer, morning time was extremely pleasing.

After the President left the White House, the staff would come alive like mice when the cat's away. With so many chores to do and all the activities the First Lady had planned on that day, there was little time to get everything in order.

The First Lady retreated to her office to call a special meeting with a few of her staff that she could rely on to research her husband's request discretely and not reveal to anyone what they were actually doing. She made it quite clear to them that this research was to be in strict confidence only to her and not to bring any attention to anyone of what they were doing. She needed only the facts on this issue and didn't need any opposition interfering with the gathering of information on this delicate matter and to have the findings documented on paper and returned to her office as soon as possible. She told them that a lot of people wanted to see the President fail on this issue and there were certain people that were financially going to be affected in a negative way and that it was imperative that this situation be handled extremely carefully. When she finished this discussion, she excused the team from her office and called her personal secretary in to go over the rest of the day's itinerary.

In the car, the President was looking over some notes. Again he was thinking about the garbage situation almost as if it were haunting him. He had done so much research on this and sat many a night in his favorite chair trying to come up with an answer. Still not clear on how to clean up the situation, he decided to jump in anyway.

As the car approached the curb, the President got out and was soon greeted by the New Jersey Senator. A longtime acquaintance, they had been friends since law school. Laughing about a joke they played on one of the Professors as they usually did whenever the two (2) were together.

"Well Sir," said the Senator. "This garbage situation that you are involved in… I received your telegram yesterday." The President puts his hand on the Senator's shoulder and says, "Gene, if you wouldn't mind, I would like to bring this entire subject up in front of all the members." With a sly grin, the Senator again spoke, "Sir, I don't know what you've got up your sleeve, but you have my support. Anything to clean up this problem would be nothing less than a miracle." The President smiles back at his friend and says, "thank you, I am glad you are on board, I need all the support I can get on this issue." Reminiscing of the "Old Law Professor" again, they started to laugh as they walked inside the building.

"All Rise", says the speaker of the house. As the National Anthem begins to play; the President and Senator Gene Baker make their way to the front of the room as the Senator turns and takes his seat leaving the President to continue walking alone toward the podium shaking hands with some of the Senators along his way.

Suddenly all is quiet as the President makes his way up the steps and walks up to the podium and speaks. "Good morning to all." As he grins. The members start to laugh. "Did I miss a joke? It is morning; at least my secretary told me it was." As the President looks at his watch; again everyone in the room laughs and this time applauds him. The President smiling back starts speaking to the members in the room. "I have called a meeting to discuss this country's waste disposal problem. I have asked Senator Baker to head up this discussion as well as the committee with the well-known situation that New Jersey had just last year. Let me introduce to you the New Committee Chairman of Waste Disposal, Senator Gene Baker of New Jersey." (All the members start to applaud). The Senator waits for the President to return to his seat before speaking. "Ladies and Gentlemen, Committee members and friends... Just last year a barge with 3100 tons of garbage embarrassing Long Island haunted the ocean waters as far south as the Gulf of Mexico in search of a place to dump. Long distance truckers haul waste from the metro region to dumps as far as West Virginia. Since this tragic and embarrassing incident has happened, a law was signed in my home state requiring homeowners to make recycling easier by separating their garbage. Glass in one container, newspapers in another, etc. New Jersey has approached the limit of its last landfill; the least glamourous of government agencies is presently the one that is most important.

In Passaic County a One Hundred and Fifteen (115,000,000) Million Dollar Incinerator is still two (2) years away. The five (5) year contract to haul waste to Johnstown, Pennsylvania which is three hundred and forty (340) miles away has been closed.

The State warned its residence over twelve (12) years ago that this day was coming and with the knowledge that we were headed for a real garbage disaster; in 1975, a law was passed holding each county responsible for the disposal of its own garbage.

Many officials feel that the State ducked its responsibilities by doing this; the fact is that the crunch will last until all of the State's individual counties finally build their own incinerators.

Most of the Northern Counties face a cost of over two (2) billion dollars for incinerators. They argue that the State should come up with ways of raising this kind of money. There is also talk of declaring a garbage emergency." The Senator pauses for a moment as the crowd starts mumbling amongst themselves. He lets it go on for a few minutes then starts to address his fellow Senators.

"Friends, Comrades, fellow Senators...this is a real physical problem that we have not addressed. We live in a throwaway society and this needs to change. This needs to change now. We have exhausted our dump sites, which has caused polluted run offs and so forth and so on. It is time to take responsibility and time for action.

We can set up recycling plants, which in turn create jobs. We can offer grants to entrepreneurs who have the ability and imagination to make actual useable products out of recycled materials, which in turn also creates jobs and puts people back to work. A returnable fee put on all recycled materials will also inspire the average tax paying citizen to turn in recycled materials to the center thereby getting money back. I remember as a child I would go along the road and woods and pick up coke bottles and turn them into the grocery store for a few pennies apiece. I was a child and the money I made bought me a few snacks and a comic book. I was happy and back then we were not so abusive to our environment. People actually repaired their televisions and radios. Now when something breaks, it is thrown away and a new one replaces it. Unfortunately, now we have landfills full of old televisions and everything else. Disposable diapers instead of cloth diapers, I can go on and on. You get the picture I am sure. So what do we do? We change, not because we want to, but because we have to." The Senator puts down the microphone and walks off the stage away from the podium. The crowd applauds as he walks back to his seat.

The Speaker of the House again presiding over Congress walks up to the podium and dismisses the audience.

The President goes into the back pressroom where a select few reporters has been waiting diligently for the meeting to end.

"Mr. President, Mr. President" as all the reporters say at the same time. "One at a time," he replies. "Stacey, New York Times right?" The President addresses her. Stacy answers, "Yes sir, my question is how do you propose to handle this large of a problem?" The President smiles and answers the group, "One day at a time." As he stops and points to another reporter. "Jerry, from Washington I believe?" Jerry answers, "Yes Sir, you spoke of entrepreneurs and grant money to create industry from recycling." The President starts shaking his head. "Yes I did, do you have any ideas that you would be interested in applying for." Everyone in the room laughs. "Mr. President, Mr. President," again everyone in the room calling his name. He points to the gentlemen in the back and says to him, "I don't know you, what is your name and where are your from." The man stands tall and speaks, "My name is Arthur and I am from England, sir...my question is actually a suggestion. In my country we have a pole tax and so people don't collect so much junk because they are taxed on it." The President pauses for a moment and says to him, "Well if you are a junk collector I guess this is the right country to live in." Everyone laughs. Then he speaks again. "Yes, I am well aware of it and you do have a point, England is a tiny country and they do not have the garbage problems that we have. It is true we live in a time where people have a compulsive obsessive necessity to purchase anything and everything, whether they need it or not. This is something that we are going to have to wean ourselves from." Pointing to the woman in the corner, "Yes, Debra from Atlanta I believe?" She answers, "Yes Sir, my question is has Congress written this bill yet and what is it going to be called so that we can follow its progress?" The President thinks for a moment then says, "The Act of '88, Senator Gene Baker will be the sponsor of this bill... and you can contact him. No more questions; have a nice day and thank you for your patience." The President turns and leaves the room.

The President looks to his administrative assistant and asks, "Well how do you think it went." Johnathon says, "Sir, excellent...and humorous too. Straight and to the point; also it was smart move to give them Senator Baker's name so that they will hound him instead of you." The President smiles and says, "You might go ahead and send him a bottle of Grey Goose and a note for me that says, "Don't get cooked." He is going to need it." The President says to Johnathon on a serious side. "Gene Baker can handle the press; I have all the confidence in the world in him. He knows what he is up against. We discussed it last week. He is the best we have on this issue, as the Senator of New Jersey he has his hand on the pulse of the problem." Johnathon replies to the President, well at least he has knowledge of it Sir. It is not like he is going in blind folded." The President looks at Johnathon and says to him. "That is why I picked Gene Baker; he is the only Senator we have that has a complete understanding of the problem."

Chapter 3

The President walks out of the building and into his limousine. "Stanford I am hungry where are we going for lunch?" Says the President. Stanford replies, "Sir you have a luncheon at the Vice President's home. The First Lady informed the chauffer's office twenty minutes ago. I am to take you there immediately. Lunch should be ready in fifteen minutes and I will have you there in ten." "Thank you Stanford." He replies and picks up the paper to read the sports page.

Pulling up to the Vice President's home where the First Lady and Charlotte, the

Vice President's wife are looking at flowers in the front garden. Stanford stops the limousine, gets out, and opens the door for the President as his bodyguard and the security team in the car behind him head toward the back door in the kitchen.

The President walking up toward the front door grabs the arm of his darling wife kissing her on her cheek and then gives a hug to Charlotte. The Vice President Dan Morgan is standing at the door and invites them all in as he says to the President, "I thought that after that meeting you could use a good meal and a little reprieve from the peanut gallery of reporters." The President laughs and says, "Actually they weren't too hard on me under the circumstances. I am starving and I know you are a beef man." The President and Vice President both start laughing, as they walk into the dining room. Enjoying a pleasant meal, they wait until after lunch and go into the study to have a drink and discuss the activities of the day and the duties that the Vice President will take on to assist the President so that he can focus his energies on other pressing matters.

"Sir it is a good thing that we have no military issues pending" says the Vice President. "You are so right," replies the President. "This is going to be a very expensive resolve and we need to focus the financial aspect of this entire program. I need you to try and keep tabs on anything that could result in a military dispute and intervene so that we can eliminate any war situation from happening this term. We cannot afford it. We need to take care of our own backyard right now. You need to let the military boys on Capitol Hill know this and stress the point." The Vice President nods his head and says, "I understand Sir." The President speaks again, "We need to take care of our Veterans and we need to also look at what kind of programs that are available to utilize the military for the enforcement of putting this bill into action. We may have some unforeseen problems when we shut down the dumps. I need you to look into this for it could be a homeland security issue as well as serious health issues, so be sure to keep in contact with the CDC." The Vice President replies, "Oh... good thinking Sir, I didn't think about the health issues that could come up." The President says to his friend, "We really don't want to bring the health issues to the front of this; we just want to keep an eye on it to prevent any disasters. We don't need a panic on our hands, you know what I mean." The Vice President nods his head. "Yes Sir, I understand completely what you are getting at." "Glad that you are on board my friend; shall we adjourn to the ladies now?" he says, as he shakes the

Vice President's hand. The Vice President replies, "sounds good to me; I will handle my end Sir." The President responds, "I know I can count on your support Dan, I do appreciate all that you do, and I want you to know that." The Vice President replies, "That is what I am here for Sir." The two (2) gentlemen leave the study and head to the patio garden for ice cream with the ladies.

Chapter 4

Across town, several of the concerned Congressmen were sitting at the local tavern talking about this situation and how it was going to affect their wealthy constituents that backed their campaigns. Congressman Wilson of Arkansas and Congressman Barrows of Oklahoma said that they did not have any problems in their State with garbage. Congressman Wilson said to the group. "This is a problem with big cities in small states. I think that this should stay on the state level not be a Federal Law." Congressman Marshall of Florida replied, "We subcontract as a

State to a large company to handle the entire waste disposal and it is part of the property taxes bill and we pay the subcontracting company at the end of the year. We have a methane plant and currently have a voluntary recycling program in place by providing the necessary bins to be used by the homeowners. For the most part the local residents do their best to recycle. We are a big state with a big population. Hurricanes are the biggest problem we have... what to do with all the damaged mess. This takes years to clean up and dispose of. I have to agree with the President boys, I think that this is a Federal problem; however, I do think that we need to address this first on a

State level. If a State can handle it then let them, otherwise if it is too much for them to handle then bring in the National Guard." The entire Congressmen start to laugh. Congressman Lacey of Vermont speaks, "We too in Vermont have recycling laws; even though we are a small State, we have a small population and I think that we can handle the problems of our own State as well. I agree with Congressman Marshall, I think that if we can handle our own State and resolve the garbage problems, we need to do it on a local ordinance, however, I know that the bigger cities are going to have some serious issues to overcome as well as expenses; let's face it we all will have our hands out for Federal money." Congressman Marshall laughs at the remark, while the entire group of Congressman began shaking their heads, as they agreed with the Vermont Congressman's statement.

Back at the White House the President and his wife were just returning from their luncheon and each went to their separate offices to address their individual schedules. As the President settles into his chair, his assistant Johnathon walks in with some papers for him to sign. He speaks, "Sir, I just wanted you to know that I was over at Bailey's Tavern for lunch and I overheard some of the Congressman talk about this garbage issue." The

President's eyebrows rise as he replies to the young assistant, "What did they say?" Johnathon responds, "Well Sir, you should know that Vermont and Florida agree with you, however, they feel that it should be a local issue should each State feel that they can resolve the issues themselves. Arkansas and Oklahoma are going to give you a problem and Senator Lacey said that everyone is going to have their hands out for Federal money... Sir." The President looks at Johnathon, "Thank you son, I know how to handle a hand out. If they want to handle it themselves then it is not a Federal Issue; they can finance it themselves. Actually that is the best news I have had. We can focus our attention on States that are in serious trouble first, then work our way down the line. I need you to set me up an appointment to meet with Congressman Marshall and Congressman Lacey separate. Make it a few days apart, go ahead, and schedule a few of the other Congressman who have small populations. This will keep them from being alarmed. I need to know how they plan on taking care of this issue on a State level. Johnathon thank you very much. This is extremely helpful. Again, you are doing a good job and I appreciate it. I'm done with this discussion."

Jonathon takes out his note pad. "Sir the next thing on your agenda is your trip to Turkey. You are scheduled to leave next week for a meeting with the Prime Minister; and then you have been invited to a party two days later for the new King of Jordan. I spoke with the First Lady's personal secretary and she will be accompanying you on this trip. The Vice President will be in Washington the entire time you are gone and as for the Secretary of State, she will also be in the Middle-East, but in Israel and Cairo on a good will trip. Sir... the world seems to be on an even keel and no-one is fighting at the moment." The President peeps his eyes over his glasses and says, "Johnathon I hope it stays that way." Johnathon says to the President, "Anything else I can do for you Sir?" The President smiles and says, "No, not that I can think of. I made notes on these documents, give them to the girls for processing and see that these papers are given priority over whatever else they are doing at the moment. That will be all." Johnathon takes the papers from the President and leaves the room.

The First Lady is sitting at the head of the Conference Room table with several members of her staff as they go over what needs to be done while she will be out of Washington traveling with her husband for the next two weeks. The First Lady speaks, "I need someone to attend a luncheon for me for the Council of Arts in New York. Please apologize for me that I had to accompany the President overseas. Secondly, I need someone to attend a ribbon cutting ceremony for the new Woman's Shelter here in Washington. The rest of the staff I need to focus at just keeping everything running smoothly until I get back, you have my schedule and can assign someone to cover for me any of the scheduled events that need to be attended by a representative to apologize for my absence. In addition, I need personal information of the wives and families of the Prime Minister and the new King of Jordan on my desk sometime by noon tomorrow. That will be all." As the First Lady excuses herself and returns to her office. Her staff stays behind and Edgar her personal secretary goes through her calendar and schedules the various personnel to each of the tasks at hand. Upon completion, he then heads for the First Lady's Office to see if she needed any assistance in packing for her trip or anything that she may need. Usually the personal secretary for the First Lady is a woman, however Edgar served the First Lady very well as a personal assistant when she was a Senator's wife so she just brought him with her to Washington since he is so professional and has such a flair for design and fashion, that she decided years ago he was just what she needed to keep her in style for the public.

The day was winding down as the President had just finished another meeting with several committee members as they went over different proposals on various issues mostly concerning budgets. The President made it perfectly clear that he needed to find the money to focus on the cost of incinerators and clean up. This was too important for the health and welfare of the country. The President says casually, "We could cut the budget for expanding military vehicles and artillery since we are not at war. The space program also could be cut since the private sector is investing in satellites, let them spend their money not the American peoples. We need to do a line item audit on the budget," the President says. "I need to know where every dime is going. We need to tighten our belts, we need to clean up our country and we need to clean up our finances as well." The entire room was silent. The President looks at Brantley at the other end of the table and says to him, "Brantley you are the head of the accounting team. When I get back from the Middle-East I need an itemized list of every dime for every department and what it is going for. You have two (2) weeks from the end of this week to get the list together. You have the budget, get with all the various department managers and get their budgets. I want it all, expenses, salaries, pensions, the whole ball of wax. Do you think you can do that?" Brantley looks at the President, "Yes Sir, it is all in the computer and I will have the whole office working on it so that you will have the budget breakdown on your desk when you get back, by dividing up the individual government programs, we can assign each of our caseworkers to different divisions of the government and that way we will have it all covered." The President smiles and then asks, "Oh Brantley I want a list of all pork barrel projects separated on a need basis." Brantley looks at the President and replies, "Yes Sir, I understand." The President stands and says to everyone in the room. "This garbage cleanup of our country is my number one task. We will do this and we will find the funding to pull this off. This is my main concern right now. We need to clean up America. Senator Gene Baker is currently writing this bill "Act of 88" and I want everyone to give him their full support on this bill. This is going to be my legacy. I will take it as a personal insult to anyone that goes against what I am trying to do for this country and for the next generation and future generations. Yes, we are going to rock some boats and some people are not going to be happy, but this is not about that. This is about doing what is right for America." Looking at his watch, the President closes the meeting for the day as he tells them it is six o'clock and past time for everyone to go home. Slowly getting up from the Conference table, the President is the first to walk out of the room while the rest of the staff talks amongst themselves on the day's events.

Chapter 5

Heading up to the Presidential Suite, several staff members make small talk with the President as he heads up the stairs. Stopping for a moment, he looks around at the pictures hanging on the walls and thinks about all the men before him and the impact that they had on the country as well as the decisions that they made and how it affected our nation. He thought about Roosevelt and how he had to deal with the financial devastation that our country was in. How he created the CCC to give jobs to our young men and put them back to work building roads and creating the park services to protect our forests. He looked at Kennedy and remembered how he stood firm on not going to war with Cuba much less Vietnam and how it cost him his life. Lincoln was known for the Abolishment of Slavery, it too cost him his life. How many Presidents stood firm in their beliefs to do what was in the best interest of the people; in the best interest of the country. He wanted to be one of them, to do what was best for his time and to clean up our country and our environment for the future generations of America. That was an honorable task.

As he headed for the Presidential suite, his wife was standing at the door with a glass of brandy for her husband.

Smiling at him she says, "Had a rough day...I can see it on your face." The President replies, "You can't imagine. I had a meeting with the budgeting staff. I need to find the funds to put this bill proposal through. I know that this cannot be done overnight, however, I think that if we set a ten (10) year goal to reduce waste by fifty (50) percent that it can be done.

The First Lady hands her husband a file folder and says to him, "I had my staff do some research and here is some information that they dug up." Suddenly the President's eyes light up as he opens the folder and takes out the first piece of paper and starts to read it, as he walks over to his chair and sits down.   Looking at the paper then looking at his wife, he says to her as he reads the document aloud. "The brunt of an American joke the garbage barge has been rejected not only by six states but three foreign countries. Awaiting its fate, this ship has proven that we are on the tip of a national garbage disaster. As the communities around the country have to face rapidly filling landfills, the municipalities are going to have to look at ways to reduce waste by promoting a reduction program by mandatory recycling and more wisely using incinerated trash for energy needs.

The barge itself has shown not only our country, but also countries around the world that we have a serious problem on the horizon. The National Conference of State Legislators recently passed a proposal on reduction at the source with specific concerns about hazardous and infectious waste.

The fact is, that it is the United States citizens that generate two times the garbage per capita than other developed countries around the world. Landfills here in this country are closing at a rapid rate due to the pollution that gradually seeps into the ground contaminating the ground water. In New York State, alone 1300 landfills have closed leaving only 300 landfills to handle the garbage. Within a year, they too will be expired with no more room.

The city of Islip agreed to take the refuse for 124 thousand dollars however, it must be inspected for hazardous and infectious waste by order of the State Judge. The barge will have to dock in Queens and then be unloaded and a truck will have to haul the refuge. When a state does not have an incinerator, it has to send its garbage to another state by truck. That is why you see so many garbage trucks on the interstates.

New Jersey has a levy against products that are packaged in disposable packaging. It is suggested that Congress needs to remove financial incentives that promote the use of throwaway and instead give the incentives to reusable packaging.

Rhode Island and New Jersey have mandated recycling programs and the State of Oregon has jumped on the Environmentally Friendly train and has passed a Recycle Act, so that its citizens separate refuse... paper, glass, cans, etc. and have it picked up by the local municipalities. The State of Florida also does the same thing, however, they have dedicated days for certain items. They even provide the containers.

What is truly needed to make this program cost efficient it to have a recovery resource system, and to burn the trash for energy. Our research shows that in Japan and in Western Europe, they are already doing this successfully with stringent environmental protection programs. Fortunately, for us, we do have the technology and there are actually ways that we can reduce hazardous wastes and emissions. The problem is that the media asks the question is it safe and that makes people nervous.

Incineration of trash without capturing energy is too costly and landfills are quickly filling to capacity so we need to look at the other options.

New York State has adopted a solid-waste management plan. Eighty (80) percent of the seventeen point five

(17.5) million tons of garbage each year is placed in depleting landfills. Twelve (12) percent is eliminated through a recovery plant. Four (4) percent is reduced through recycling and four (4) percent is shipped out of state to be incinerated. The State has a goal of eliminating waste by reduction and recycling within the next ten (10) years with forty (40) percent processed through a recovery resource, however this is still to be seen. This factual information was retrieved through an article that was in the Christian Science Monitor on May 20, 1987. It is obvious that some of the larger states are realizing that time is running out and they are looking for ways to intervene in the obvious catastrophic problem that is headed their way. The bottom line is that our throwaway society is running out of land to put the throwaway stuff. It is imperative that we as a nation downsize and become more aware of what we are buying and start fixing what it is that we are throwing away in order to buy the upgraded item that we just threw away. When you think about it how wasteful, we are as well as it is financially stupid on your pocket book. Washington needs to look in the mirror as well. What are we as the leaders of the nation doing to show the rest of the country that we as well need to be cutting out wasteful spending on items that only fill up the landfills? We need to be on the front line setting an example.

In third world countries, they have markets where people shop for fresh goods. Whereas in most of the country here; we have chain food stores, the frozen food section of the grocery store is full of throwaway containers for customer convenience. Unfortunately, it is obvious that modern convenience is a big cause of the problems that we are now suffering from. There are a few small communities that have farmers markets. In some of the small farming towns in Oregon, you actually go to the baker for bread, the butcher for eggs and meat, the dairy farm for milk, cheese and butter, and the produce market for your vegetables. The food is fresh and there is very little waste, especially if you bring your own containers. Through time and convenience over the years, we as a nation have gotten lazy and wasteful and it is a habit that has escalated to the point that it is now a severe problem that will bring with it health issues that could cause massive illnesses and even death. The only resolve is to change our thought process and our spending habits by being more conservative as well as environmentally conscious and only purchasing that which we need; not being such a glutinous society. What is most important of all it to put a ban on barges that carry trash on our seas. In essence what we need is for the Garbage Barge Bill to actually be a Trash Free Seas Bill."

The President looks at the First Lady and says to her, "I have to commend your staff; they really did a good job on their initial research. It will be interesting to see what else they come up with in the next month. There are definitely some good material facts that we can use in formulating the bill to present to Congress. Let your team know that I am pleased. I especially liked the part about the incentives to the States that are pushing the products in recycled and recyclable packages and I like what they said about Trash Free Seas, this is really important because this is something that we can take with us overseas on our trip and discuss this with the other countries as well." The First Lady smiles and replies back, "I am glad that you are pleased. I know that we have a lot of work to do. I have asked my staff to work on a list of items that could possibly go into the bill and to forward it to Senator Gene Baker for his review." The President shakes his head and says, "Yes...I think that is a good idea. We don't need to be micro managing everything and besides we will be out of town and they can get a jump on this while we are gone."

Suddenly there is a knock on the door. The President gets up to see who it is. The President's security team is standing outside the door with a man from the courier service that is holding a large envelope marked CONFIDENTIAL in large black letters. "Excuse me sir, I was told to deliver this to you immediately from Senator Baker." The President takes the envelope from the young man thanking him and closes the door. Walking back to his chair, he sits down and opens the envelope and pulls out a letter with the few pages that are stapled. The letter is marked in bold black letters DRAFT, as he reads the letter.

Dear Mr. President, I am sending you a preliminary update of the Senate Bill S.0088 The Garbage Barge Bill – Act of '88 for your review. Due to your interest in this matter, I wanted to keep you in the loop of the progress that we are making as we proceed with the passing of this particular Bill. My staff as well as several other Senators that are on the Committee have been extremely helpful in acquiring information and having their staff as well do research on this particular subject. I have found that we can take this Bill to encompass several pending issues that need to be addressed as well. The more research that we do, the more things that are coming up that are environmentally potential hazards that I feel are important to include in this Bill. It is important that we get everything in this Bill that pertains to the issues that we are addressing and that we get it right the first run for it will save time and money as well as to keep this from being put on the back burner for other pending bills that are not as important to you as this one is. I will inform you as we will be updating with new data as it becomes available as well as adding the concerns of onshore waste as well.

Senator Gene Baker, D-NJ

GB/dd

cc/Senate/Congress,

bcc/U.S. President

S.0088 – Garbage Barge Bill - Act of '88

A bill to authorize and improve the Marine Debris Research, Prevention, and Reduction Act, and for other purposes such as recycling, incinerators, in reducing land waste and pollutants that eventually end up in our oceans.

Sponsor

Senator Gene Baker, D-NJ

Committees

Senate Committee of Commerce, Science, and Transportation

Related Issue Areas

Environmental protection

Heath

Coast guard

Official Summary

Garbage Barge - Act of '88. (Sec. 2) For trash free seas, to create a Marine Debris Research, Prevention, and Reduction Act to state a purpose of such Act to address the adverse effects of overloaded landfills and impacts of debris on the marine environment, safety of navigation and the economy of the country through research and identification of source.

Organizations Supporting S.0088

Green Peace

Save our Oceans

Organizations Opposing S.0088

None at this time.

Latest Letters to Congress

I am writing as a constituent in the 15th Congressional district of from the State of Georgia in regards to the Act of '88. Please support this bill.

Garbage Barge Bill – Act of '88

A bill to authorize and improve the Marine Debris Research, Prevention through the Reduction Act of Land Waste, and for other purposes

To name this Program, the Marine Debris Prevention and Removal Program and to include the Administrator of the National Oceanic and Atmospheric Administration (NOAA) to undertake marine research and assessment and reduction and prevention efforts, with a focus on debris posing a threat to both land and living marine resources, in the marine environment, navigational safety and/or the U.S. economy including:

81

(1) Research and assessment of derelict fishing and gear;

(2) Research and assessment of plastics, with respect to the health of the marine environment;

(3) The establishment of a process for maintaining an inventory of the types and impacts of marine debris found in the navigable waters of the United States and the U.S. exclusive economic zone (EEZ);

(4) Measures to identify the origin, location, and projected movement of marine debris within U.S. navigable waters, the EEZ and the high seas. Requires the Administrator to undertake efforts to prevent, reduce,

and remove the occurrence and impacts of marine debris, including the adverse impacts of boats, commercial barges, derelict fishing gear, including by;

(1) Working with all other related agencies to address land-based sources that end up as marine debris.

(2) conduct research and development of alternatives to materials, shipping crates, and/or gear posing threats to the marine environment and methods for making gear used in specific fisheries to enhance the tracking, recovery, and identification of lost and discarded materials, shipping crates, and/or gear;

(3) Conduction research related to shoreline resiliency to marine debris impacts for purposes of navigational safety, protecting living marine resources and the marine environment, or protecting the U. S. economy.

(4) developing effective no regulatory measures and incentives to cooperatively reduce the volume of lost and discarded materials, shipping crates, fishing gear and to aid in its recovery;

(5) Developing interagency action plans for the preparation for, and timely response to, a severe marine debris event;

(6)   carrying out research relating to assessing the potential economic impacts of severe marine debris events on the economies of coastal states, including impacts to fishing, shipping, transportation,   aquaculture, ecotourism, and other industries;

(7)   developing and implementing strategies, methods, priorities, and a plan for tracking, preventing, and removing marine debris that is in, or likely to enter, U.S. navigable waters or the EEZ, including the development of local or regional protocols for removal of materials, shipping crates, derelict fishing gear and other marine debris.

(8) Providing national and regional coordination to assist states, Indian tribes, and regional organizations in addressing local land and marine debris issues.

(9) Promoting international action to reduce the incidence of both land marine debris; and

(10) Developing and disseminating tools and products related to such activities. Requires the Administrator to undertake outreach and education of the public and other stakeholder, such as the shipping industry, fishing industry, fishing gear manufacturers, other marine-dependent industries, and

the plastic and waste management industries, on;

(1)   Sources of debris;

(2)   Sources of marine debris from overburdened landfills;

(3)   Threats associated with marine debris; and

(4)   Approaches to identify, determine sources of, assess, reduce, remove, and prevent marine debris and its adverse impacts on the marine environment, navigational safety, and the U.S. economy.

Official Summery

The Garbage Barge Bill – Act of '88

As the President hands the document to his wife; The First Lady looks it over and says to her husband. "Well dear, it looks like your campaign promise is making headway! This document covers quite a bit of the problems at hand. It is not just about trash, it is also about the environmental waters of not only our country but also others. This would be a good document to take with you as you visit the Prime Minister of Turkey. I would think that he would be interested in this as well. I wonder how they handle their waste management problems in Turkey and Jordan as well. This good will trip could benefit the whole global community by talking about these issues. It is a future problem for everyone, everywhere. Don't you agree?" The President gets up from his chair and looking at his wife says, "You are right on target. I agree completely with what you are saying. This is a good idea that we can share with them. I am sure that they too have issues and it would be great to all be on the same page throughout the world. It is a growing problem that I am sure is on everyone's mind. Especially in this soon to be global economy, that appears to be headed that way."

Sara the cook comes out of the kitchen and puts dinner on the table for the President and the First Lady. As she pops her head into the den where the two of them are sitting to let them know that their supper is ready in the formal dining room and that she is done for the evening, as she wishes them a good night.

The President and the First Lady get up and both head for the dining room and have a nice quiet meal for the evening with small talk about anything but politics. After dinner, the President as usual takes the plates into the kitchen and he washes the dishes as she dries them. Whereas most of the Presidents' have staff to do this; this President said he and The First Lady (his wife), preferred to do it themselves. "It keep us in touch with reality" he said, when he was first elected and spoke with the private Presidential staff to instruct them how things were to be handled in the President's private suite. He let everyone know that there were certain tasks that he preferred to do himself. When he was in their private suite, he wanted his life to be as normal as possible. "After all" he said to his staff, "one day this will all be over and I need to know how to function as a regular guy." The staff all laughed at his sense of humor. He and the First Lady both had a good relationship with all of the staff members.

The evening was over and the President and the First Lady having finished doing the dishes and cleaning up the kitchen, retired to their bedroom for a well-deserved goodnights rest.

Chapter 6

The next morning came and after eating at the breakfast table, the President and the First Lady go their separate ways.

Walking down the stairs the First Lady is met with several of her security to take her to her first appointment to meet with the Washington, D.C. School Board and discuss the needs for foreign languages in Primary School.

As they drive up to the Administrative Building, she gets out of the car along with her entourage of staff and security and they walk down the hallway to the packed auditorium. The First Lady walks up to the podium as the audience give a big applause. She pauses a moment until the room quiets then starts to address the crowd. "Good Morning to all," she says. "I am pleased that so many of you are as concerned as I am that here in this country, most of our children only speak one language. The President and I were in the Dominican Republic last year and the elementary age children in this small island country speak between three (3) to five (5) languages; whereas the middle and high school students speak somewhere between five(5) to seven (7) languages."

You can hear the crowd gasp...Suddenly the crowd starts whispering among themselves. The First Lady just lets this go on for about five minutes then again the room gets quiet.

She starts to speak again. "Yes...that is right; this small impoverished country has absolutely no illiteracy. The education system in this country in languages is far above our standards, as is most of the Caribbean Islands. Due to the fact that there is little opportunity for work on these tiny tourist destination islands. The schools provide the students with languages in order for them to move forward with their lives and careers where they need to go in order to provide for themselves and a family. With a global economy on the horizon, it is imperative that we too as a country prepare for this and prepare our children as well for we do not know what the future holds and technology is changing things so fast that we need to be prepared; especially our children. The fact is all over the world, everyone speaks our language; but here in this country, very few speak other languages and I feel that this needs to change."

The First Lady again pauses as the audience once again applauds. As she picks up the microphone and says, "We need to do what is in the best interest for the future generations of America. Language is how we communicate with one another. By teaching our children how to speak other languages, we can give them the tools to speak and work with others from other countries and keep our jobs intact here in this country as we as a nation expand our global economy... Thank you for your support."

As the First Lady steps down from the podium and speaks with several of the members of the Washington school board as well as the many guests that have questions on the funding of such a task. She meanders around shaking hands and tells them that they will find a way to support the foreign language teachers somehow. Stopping in front of her limousine, with her secretary and her security team, the journalists surround her with their camera's pointing. She graciously says to them,

"If in poor depressed countries they can afford to teach their children to speak several languages, there is no reason that we can't do it here." As she steps into the car, the crowd cheers, and they drive off.

Edgar addresses the First Lady, "Madam, you did a fabulous job addressing the issue at hand; I have to tell you...you really told them how important it was to the future of their children, not to be globally illiterate." The First Lady looks at Edgar and says, "I like that terminology, you should have put that word into my script. We will have to use it more often. I like that word, Globally Illiterate! That is a powerful way of putting this across. We need to put that out there. Be sure to contact your source at US Today and let's use that in the next article they do on education." Edgar smiling at the First Lady says, "Yes Madam, I will be sure to take care of that for you."

As he takes a small yellow note, pad out of his briefcase and writes it down.

The President is sitting in his office with a few members of his staff going over the itinerary of things to be handled while he is on his overseas trip, when Brantley walks into the room with his hands full of file folders.

The President excuses the staff and asks Brantley to have a seat in front of his desk as he gets up from the couch and heads towards the desk chair and the crowd clears out of the room closing the door.

"Brantley," the President says to him. "Please have a seat and make yourself comfortable." (As Brantley wiggles a little in the chair to get settled.) Again the President speaks, "What have you found out so far about cutting items so that we can finance incinerators for the larger cities?" Brantley taking some papers out of the top file folder. "Well sir... I have some good news for you...We can cut some spending on foreign aid that I know is financing the gunrunners in several countries. We have plenty of ammunition stockpiled and do not need to be spending more military money on bullets. With today's technology, ground teams can be cut back. In addition, the Department of Education is spending a lot of money on new Administrative Buildings that really do not have anything to do with teaching students. However, I also do not really want to use that pot of money because I was saving that one for the First Lady's foreign language fund. She and I were in a meeting the other day as well for her needs to find the funding for her education project. We could put a hold on all Federal Government raises on salaries and pensions for a year and we can cut out several stupid grant funds that are truly a waste of money. I found several thousand of them. We have over five hundred grants that give money for everything from researching prostitution in foreign countries to the mating rituals of peacocks. Sir, I think that we need to take a serious look and audit the grant books." The President starts to snicker..."Yes Brantley," he says as he continues to laugh, " I think that you are right, we do need to have a team go through this item by item." Brantley looks firmly at the President and says, "Sir, I thought you would say that and I have my office working on it as we speak." The President shaking his head says to Brantley, "Peacocks huh... what they will think of next." Brantley replies, "Sir, I would like to know who approved it personally." The

President replies, "Me too... Well Brantley, you have your work cut out for you, get the numbers together for me and we will get back with this after my trip. Thank you and you can be excused. Tell the girls to have something sent in for lunch for two, General Canton will be here in half an hour and I am getting a little hungry. Grilled salmon sandwiches would be fine. I know that the General is a fish man; he goes to Alaska every year. They know the routine. Thank you again Brantley."

Brantley leaves the office and gives the President's order to the girls in the next room who make arrangements for the President and the General's meal.

Chapter 7

Sitting at his desk, the President looks at the pile of papers he has to sign and goes to reading. The cat under his feet starts to play with the tassels on his loafers as he takes his foot and pushes the cat away. Looking down under his desk he reaches down and picks up the cat and gets up and carries the cat over to the window sill and puts the cat on it as he says to the cat, "We are having fish for lunch so you might want to be on your best manners old boy." Walking back to his desk, he sits back down and goes back to reading and putting his initials and post it notes on the documents for the office staff to take care of.

Before too long the General walks in with one of the secretaries who has several bags of food and sets the table near the window overlooking the rose garden for lunch for both the President and the General, as they sit down and enjoy a meal together.

Afterwards the President says to the General, "We are going to need to cut some spending. We are not at war and we need to go over some budget issues that will not affect the morale of the Veterans. We are not at war at the moment and we can cut recruiting down a bit. Those who have served twenty years need to retire; I don't see a need for them to stay for thirty years. We are not at war and should we have a need to do a recall, we can deal with that when the need arises. I need you to handle this carefully. Our Veterans are very important to me and they have given their lives for their country, so we need to handle this with the utmost courtesy. I don't want to touch the funding for their benefits, I just need the ones who have served their time to go ahead and retire. After all, they deserve it and it will reduce some of the military budget that I need to divert to building incinerators for this garbage problem that we need to address. Do you have anything to bring to the table in regards to cutting?" The General smiles and says, "Actually I have some ideas that I would like to run by you. We as you know have many technological patents that we could let loose that are not a homeland security issue. By partnering with some of the private tech companies, we could actually bring in a substantial amount of money. Our research and development team could just about support their own budgets by doing this and it would free up enough money that you could finance the Bill for this cleanup situation that you are concerned about." The President is stunned. "Mr. President, are you alright," the General says to him. The

President shakes his head for a moment and replies, "You mean to say that all this time, we could have been doing this and saving the taxpaying citizens money?" The General says, "Yes Sir, we have all sorts of patents of various things that could be used in the civilian market that we could joint venture." The President smiling says, "Well I'll be damned. Get me the list and let's get to work. Schedule a meeting with your staff and Brantley immediately. I will give him a call this afternoon and fill him in. This is the best news I have had in a long time. It is about time that we run this country like a business. Matter of fact I think I need to address the Nation on this new State of Affairs. This is a good thing. It will create jobs here in this country. We need to be sure that we only contract this joint venture with companies that will manufacture in this country. That needs to be in the contract do you understand?" The General nodding his head, "Yes Sir Mr. President, I understand and agree completely. I am glad I can be of service Sir." The President stands up and says, "Well I think that we have completed our business General. I will be looking forward to getting together with your department when I get back and we can go over the details of what we are going to do and the bidding process." The General gets up and shakes the President's hand and replies, "Till then

Sir, I will see you when you get back from your trip." The General walks out of the room and closes the door behind him. The President does a little jig around the room; he is so excited as he looks around to make sure that no-one sees him. Picking up the phone, he tells Shelly one of the secretaries to get ahold of Brantley and have him give him a call or stop by if he is close by. Then he says her, "call Senator Baker of New Jersey and tell him I need to speak with him immediately. Also, contact the First Lady and let her know that I will be finishing up early today and to schedule dinner with the Vice President and his wife for six o'clock if he is available. Then call the media for a

State of Address statement that I need to make on a new State of Affairs that will affect this country in a positive way. Set it up for nine o'clock tonight." Shelly writing everything down replies to the President, "Yes sir, I have it all written down and am taking care of it all as we speak Sir...is there anything else I can do for you Sir?" The President replies, "Oh... yes I need someone to clean up the table if you don't mind?" Shelly replies, "I'll send someone in right away Sir." The President hangs up the phone and Jonathon walks in to clean up the table after the President's luncheon with the General.

Johnathon addresses the President, "Sir you look extremely pleased today. I take it you had a nice lunch with the General?" The President smiling replies, "Matter of fact I did Johnathon, and it is a whole new ball game now son and we are going to rock the house and run this country like a business."

"Are you speaking in Confidence Sir?" asks Johnathon. The President responds, "Yes I am. Keep in under your hat and watch the news tonight." Johnathon picking up the tray of dishes says to the President, "I will be looking forward to it Sir; anything else I can do for you?" The President replies, "No Johnathon that will be all."

As Johnathon walks out, Senator Baker and Brantley walk into the President's office. The President asks both the Gentlemen to have a seat. " I have some very good news to share with both of you," the President says as he continues, "I just had a meeting with General Canton and apparently our Military has patents that can be joint ventured into the civilian marketplace that are not a homeland security issue. There is enough money that the Research and Development Department of the Military can support themselves and we can also benefit from this by creating jobs, industry, technology, manufacturing here in this country. This will also benefit us in financing the

S.0088 Bill. I wanted the two of you to both know about this before I go and Address the Nation at nine o'clock tonight to let them know of the plans we have. I am going to do an Executive Order this afternoon and we are going to run this Country like a business...

I would appreciate it if you would keep this quiet for the moment. We are going to take the Nation by surprise tonight. Watch our ratings go through the roof boys, it is a whole new ballgame." Brantley looks at the President and asks, "Do you still want me to continue making a list of cuts in the grant book?" The President replies, "Yes I do, we are going to get out the broom and clean the house. It is time to balance the budget son. We are going to clean up America. One street at a time if we have to." Senator Baker says to the President, "Does this mean we need to wrap up the S.0088, and send it to the House Sir?" The President smiling says, "That is exactly what we need to do. If you can get it done this week I would greatly appreciate it." Senator Baker says to the President, "Done deal Sir, I'll have it typed up and we will discuss it tomorrow and hopefully get it approved in the Senate and on your desk by Friday morning." The President stands up and dismisses the two men. Outside of the President's office, it is buzzing like a beehive. The phones are ringing off the walls. You can hear all the chatter of voices asking what is going on and no-one has any answers. Johnathon on one line saying to the reporter that just called. "Sir I don't know anything other than the President has called for a State of Address at nine o'clock this evening. It will be held in the Oval Office.

The President standing at the door watching all the commotion and looking at Shelly asks her to grab a pen and paper and come into his office. She immediately forwards her phone and walks into the President's office. "How can I be of assistance Sir?" she asks. The President replies, "I need to write a speech and I need you to type me up an Executive Order. " I am ready when you are Sir." As the President replies, "The speech will give you the information that you need for the contents of the Executive Order. I need this done right away before nine o'clock tonight. Can you stay and get this done while I am at dinner with the Vice President?" Shelly nods, "Yes Sir, I will personally take care of it Sir."

She sits on the couch with pen and paper as she writes down what the President says. When he finishes, she gets up and tells him that she will get right on it and will have it all done by the time he needs it that evening, as she walks out of the room.

Looking at his watch, he pops his head out to the staff office and lets them know that he is leaving his office and heading up to the Presidential Suite and is not to be disturbed until after eight o'clock.

Walking out the door and heading down the hall nodding and shaking hands along the way, he finally makes his way to his personal residence.

The First Lady greets him with a glass of Brandy and tells him that she had his clothes laid out if he wanted to take a quick shower after he unwound that he had plenty of time. Sitting in his favorite chair with drink in hand, he took a long sigh and closed his eyes for a moment just to enjoy the solitude.

The First Lady leaves the room to give the President some quiet time as she goes into her bedroom and looks in her closet for a different pair of shoes that are a little more comfortable.

About fifteen minutes later the President walks in their bedroom to get ready for their evening with the Vice President and his wife.

"Ring...Ring...Ring" as the phone rings. The First Lady answers the phone, "Hello". Stanford is on the other line. "Yes Ma-am, let the President know that I am downstairs whenever he is ready." She replies, "We will be down in thirty minutes." Stanford answers, "That will be fine Ma-am."

Putting down the phone, she picks up a list she had started of everything that she will need to pack to go on their overseas trip. Thinking to herself, it will be nice to just get away and unwind. Knowing that the trip to Turkey will be a little hectic; she is excited about going to Jordan because it will be a private party and the press is absolutely forbidden at these affairs; also the women will be in a different area then the men because of the culture. Edgar picked up some beautiful silk scarves for the First Lady to wear on her trip and suggested that she wear them as a show of respect for their traditions. She thought to herself, "He thinks of everything, I don't know what I would do without him." As she picks them up out of the box, that was lying on the table near the bedroom door admiring them. About that time, the President peeps around the corner watching his wife and says to her, "Those are beautiful, where on earth did they come from?" She replies, "Edgar picked them up for me, they are from a little shop in Japan. He has friends over there and he advised me to wear them when we go overseas." The President says, "Smart boy you have there, not a bad idea." Again his wife replies back to him, "That is why I hired him, as she pauses for a moment then continues to speak, "Well dear if you are ready we can leave." The President hands his wife his tie and says, "Please do the honors dear, you know I can't do this." She laughs a minute then takes the tie and puts it around his neck, as they both walk out the door and down the stairs toward the door where Stanford is waiting for the two of them.

Driving around the corner, the President and his wife are quiet. It had been a long day and neither of them had much to say. Stanford kept peeking his eyes in the rear view mirror however, he too kept quiet. As they drove up to the driveway of the Vice President's residence and got out of the car, the President said to Stanford to go ahead and take a dinner break. It would be at least two hours before he would be needed.

Stanford nods his head and says thank you to the President and waits for the President and the First Lady to go into the house before he drives off leaving the security guards outside.

Standing with the door open the Vice President invites the President and his wife in, as they head toward the parlor for drinks and conversation.

Chapter 8

Across town, several of the Congressman and Senators are sitting down at the local tavern discussing this Presidential Address as they ask each other what is going on. All of Washington is in a stir with this unexpected move. Rumors are flying which is a usual thing in Washington, although no-one knows anything about this change of events that the whole country will find out at the same time. He is planning on using the element of surprise so that no-one can under mind his success for the staff was sworn to secrecy.

Charlotte takes Alex (First Lady) upstairs to give her a gift for her middle-east trip as the men have a brandy in the parlor before dinner. As Charlotte hands Alex a beautifully wrapped box, she opens it and inside is a black and beige silk tunic with matching pants. Alex looks over at her friend and gives her a big hug and thanks her as she says, "This is perfect for the party in Jordan, and I even have a scarf that will go with it. Thank you so much Charlotte, this really is too much." Charlotte smiling says to her friend, "when I saw it I thought of you and how it would be just the thing to wear over there." Alex replies, "You are right it is just the right outfit." Both the women start to giggle as they head out of the room and down the stairs to join their husbands. Alex makes a stop at the front door and hands the box to the security guard that is standing there so that she doesn't forget it later that evening.

The President and his friend Dan (Vice President) are discussing the President's plan to try and get the unnecessary spending down without creating a panic to the economy. His main concern though is getting a handle on all the trash that has piled up over the years in the landfills. The President says to Dan, "This garbage barge is really a wakeup call. This whole Country is out of control; we have become a throwaway society in every aspect. This has got to change. We need to be accountable as leaders to show by our actions. How can we tell the people to be accountable when those that run the Country are not accountable for their actions? We need to clean up our house first, and then as we go down the line, we clean up until we reach the foundation of garbage that we have accumulated. We need some common sense economics." Dan (Vice President) speaks, "I agree with you sir, but this is not a pretty subject. It is good that you are leaving for your overseas trip soon, it will be interesting to see what the other Countries are doing about this." The President shaking his head says, "I agree, this trip is important and the timing could not be better. With all the buzz going on in this town, I really am going to shake up a lot of people with this speech. I decided to leave tomorrow and take an undisclosed side trip to calm my nerves before we head out." Dan looks at the President, "Are you going to Camp David?" The President looks at his friend. "Yes, but that is between you and me. I haven't even mentioned this to the First Lady yet. I will let her know after the speech. She is pretty much packed anyway and I'm easy. A few shirts, suits, ties and miscellaneous stuff is all I need. Oh yes, maybe a turban or two." The two men start to laugh as the women are standing at the doorway letting them know that dinner is ready.

Charlotte says, "What is this about a turban?" Dan looks at his wife and says, "It's a private joke. Put on your Burka woman." Charlotte raises her eyebrows and replies, "Wrong Country Dear!" As all four of them start to laugh, they head into the dining room for a pleasant meal and lighthearted conversation. Charlotte says to Alex (First Lady), "so are you going to do a lot of jewelry shopping? I heard that the gold in Turkey is exquisite?" Alex replies, "Yes, matter of fact I am. Did you know that when you buy gold that they put it on a scale and weigh it and that is the price? I wish they would do that here; and the color is beautiful, all the jewelry is 22 to 24 karat. They also have lapis over there; I just love the deep blue color of lapis." The President jumps in and says, "Yes dear it matches the color of your eyes." Dan looks over at the President, "brownie points sir...brownie points." Charlotte says to her husband, "that's right Dan and you could use some of that yourself." Everyone at the table starts laughing. Charlotte says to the President, "I heard that the Press was not allowed at the private functions in Jordan, is that true?" The President replies, "Yes...This is a private party and they are absolutely banned from this event. Freedom of speech is an American right. In the Middle-East they have different laws and cultures than we do over here. Matter of fact, they separate the men and women at these functions. Introductions are in order and then the men go in one direction and the women go in another. There are even two dining rooms. Although I was told that we were going to be entertained by belly dancers." As he winks at his wife and wiggles his eyebrows. Alex (First Lady) comes back at him, "Don't get too excited dear, we don't want you having a heart attack or something. Remember your blood pressure." Again everyone at the table laughs. Finishing up his meal Dan says to all, "well shall we retire to the parlor for some coffee?" The President pushing his plate away says, "That sounds good to me; I need to digest all this food before I give my speech tonight. Thank you for the wonderful dinner Charlotte, you really outdid yourself this time." Alex shaking her head, "yes Charlotte you are a wonderful cook, we really appreciate this." Dan strutting like a proud peacock says, "That's why I married the girl." Charlotte looking at him replies, "Honey, you don't look like you are missing any meals." The President laughs so hard that tears come out of his eyes and says to Dan, "You don't have a chance, I don't know who her ghostwriter is but you need to hire him. She comes back with something every time." Dan just looks at the President and says, "She doesn't need any help, she is a quick draw McGraw. Her daddy was from Texas and he is just as sharp and witty." As one of the housekeepers brings in a silver tray with coffee and sits it down on the bar, she excuses herself. Alex goes over and pours herself and the President a cup of coffee as well as for Charlotte and Dan. They all sit down to digest their full bellies and enjoy the rest of their time together.

Before you know it one of the security guards knocks on the door to let the President know it is time for them to head back. Saying their goodbyes, they head out to the limousine, then off to the White House. Pulling up to the gate the President tells Stanford to go around to the back entrance as he sees all the Press at the front of the building lining up.

Slipping in the back, the President has a little time to himself before going out to address the crowd. Johnathan walks into the room with a vanilla envelope in hand and says, "Sir, I was told to give you this as soon as you got back; also the meeting has been changed to the grand ballroom to handle all the people who showed up unexpectedly for your State of Address speech." The President takes the large envelope and says to Johnathan, "Thank you and tell my secretary I appreciate her expedience and the discrete handling in this matter." Johnathan replies, "That's our job sir; is there anything else you need sir?" The President shakes his head and says, "No...that will be all. I just need to sit down and read this to myself before I read it to the world. Thank you again son, I appreciate all the hard work that you all do." Johnathon excuses himself and leaves closing the door behind him.

Opening up the envelope, the President takes the document out and sits down and glances over his speech. No sooner than he finishes, his wife comes into the room to let him know that it is time. Brushing the hair off his forehead and straightening up his tie, she walks out with him down the hallway to the grand ballroom where he will give his speech. A podium has been set up in the far right corner next to a doorway for easy exit access for the President.

Chapter 9

The room is full of Congressmen, Senators and their spouses as well as the Media. The crowd is buzzing with all sorts of conversation. The President comes into the room from the left side as the music starts playing the usual Presidential anthem. Suddenly everyone cheers and then starts clapping. The President walks between the two rows down a red carpet toward the podium as he shakes hands with those along the walkway making short conversation.

As he reaches the podium, he places both of his hands on it and the room becomes quiet. Taking his speech out of the envelope, he puts it on top of the desktop next to the microphone.

Rocking his head back and forth from all the tension he says, "Well, I am glad to see that siesta is over." Everyone laughs. The President again speaks. "You know in some Countries they go home and nap in the middle of the day and then go back to work in the evenings. No five o'clock traffic; what do you think of that." At that, the crowd starts clapping. The President just smiles and stands there for a moment. When the room again gets quiet, he starts speaking again. "Well, isn't this fun? You have no idea of why I brought you here. Curiosity is a funny thing."

Again, the crowd starts clapping. The President smiling at the audience. "On a serious note, I guess I had better get the show on the road." The crowd starts cheering for about five minutes and then again silence.

The President starts talking, "Due to recent information I have just received. We have several patents, with the Department of the Military that are not a homeland security issue. It is in the best interest financially for the Country to open up this opportunity to market these products that have been patented. These products can be utilized by a joint market venture that we are going to open up to civilian businesses that will create jobs, industry, technology, and manufacturing here in this Country."

Suddenly everyone in the room starts clapping.

The President reaches his hands out gesturing everyone to be silent. Again, the room gets quiet as the President looks around the room scanning all the faces that he knows, as he starts back at his speech. "The financial benefit of this is that the Research and Development Department of the Military will be self-sufficient and not a tax payers burden and dependent on Government Funding."

Again, the audience starts clapping and again the President   puts his hands out to get control back of the crowd.

 He begins again, "I would appreciate it if you would hold your applause until I am finished or this speech will take us to sunrise."   As the crowd laughs, he takes a moment then continues on. "Thank you, also I have notified Senator Gene Baker that we should now be able to acquire the funding for Senate Bill S.0088, The Garbage Barge Bill.   Not only are we in the process of passing this Bill. We are now going to clean up America, one street at a time if need be."

Again, the audience starts clapping. The President shaking his head starts speaking again. "We are asking each State to take responsibility for cleaning up the landfills and to build incinerators and set up recycling plants. Those larger cities that have real issues funding these projects, we will work with them. The smaller communities we will also help if they get into a bind, however this is not a handout; this is a hand up by helping those that are helping themselves. I have notified our Accounting Department to do a page-by-page audit on the Grant Book in order to get rid of Grant Money that is a waste to taxpayers and whereas there is, no benefit to what research is being done for the Grant Money.

We are asking the twenty year Veterans to retire and enjoy the rest of their lives for they have retirement and benefits of pension, medical and education. I see no need to extend the thirty year service anymore. It is time that we take the bull by the horns and clean house."

Suddenly the entire room is cheering and clapping. The President starts speaking again. It is time we get out the dust pan and clean up American."

Again, the crowded room is clapping and cheering on the President. When the room finally quiets down the

President says, "I'll fill you in with the details as we progress. You all can go home now. Thank you." As he exits the room, you can hear all sorts of conversations in the expansive room. As always, Washington is buzzing even more than usual.

In a small room of select press the President walks in to answer a few questions. Mr. President, Mr. President they all say. The President points to the woman in the back, "Stacy, New York Times what is your question?" "Thank you sir, "When is this going to take place the letting go of patents?" The President replies, "Well I have a two week trip over seas and nothing is going to happen until I get back.

Mr. President, Mr. President again the news crew all anxious to have their questions answered. The President again points over to the other side of the room. "Jerry from Washington, hello what is your question?" Jerry replies, "Thank you sir, my question is the money sir, how is the money going to be divided?" The President stands still for a moment and says, "This will be a 50/50 deal with the awarded business contractor developing the product. Fifty percent will go to the awarded contractor and fifty percent will go to the military's apportioned cause; after all it is the research and development of the military whose budget we are cutting and this money is the reward for their technology so that they can continue with their research without having the taxpayers paying for it. We need to run our financial affairs like every other business by showing accountability for what we are spending and I intend on doing this." Mr. President, Mr. President the news reporters again shouting as the President points to the woman in front of him; "I have never met you, and your question is?" "Yes sir, my name is Savanna and I am from Savanna, Georgia. My question is the cut backs on grants; is this immediate or will this be gradual?" The President smiles and says, "Good question...this will be a phase out process. Once the grant has expired, the funding will not be renewed. We do not want a total collapse and those who are currently working funded by grant money; this will give them the needed time to look for other civilian funding for their causes. Thank you for your time." As the President leaves the room surrounded by his security staff he directly heads toward his personal residence to let the First Lady know that they will be leaving first thing in the morning for Camp David for a few days to unwind before the long trip to Istanbul, Turkey and then to Jordan.

The President was glad that this part was over; he knew he had a lot on his plate to deal with when he got back, however he figured that he would let the rats hang themselves while he was gone. Going around the corner to the back stairway to the private residence, who was standing their but his good friend and confidant Senator Tom Edwards of Kentucky. "Fancy meeting you here", the President says. The Senator replies back with, "I thought that you would take the back entrance; I just needed a moment of your time before you head out of the Country." The President had stopped and said to the Senator, "Walk with me." So the two of them conversed for a few minutes over the problems that the Senator expected to be hurdles that would have to be dealt with. The

President says to the Senator, "I know when I am gone; there are people in this town that think this money is going to be a free for all. That is absolutely wrong. I am not freeing up this money so that it can go to the General Fund or to substitute it for money to be replaced that will go to the General Fund. I know how these cats work and I am relying on you to be sure that they don't hide anything in bills that will attach this new found funding to whatever scheme they are up to, to be presented to Congress while I am away. Do you understand what I am talking about?" The Senator says to the President, "I know exactly what you are saying Sir, and I agree with you completely."

Arriving at the back staircase the President shakes the Senator's hand and they part ways as the security team escorts the President to his private residence.

Once inside the President kicks off his shoes and rests in his favorite chair and nods off for a few minutes. Asleep he does not hear the First Lady walk in a little while later. She sees him sleeping and just stands there and smiles for a short time. He looks so peaceful she hates to wake him up and decides to finish packing up what she plans on taking on her trip not knowing that they are leaving the next morning.

The President's cell phone rings and it wakes him up. Looking at the number, he decides not to take the call as he gets up out of his chair and looks for his wife to let her know of the plans he made to leave early.

Finding her in her closet, he tells her that they are going to Camp David in the morning early and to please have one of the staff assist her in packing his things.

Calling her office to see if Edgar is still around, she luckily catches him before he is out the door; she was banking on him staying late for she knew he usually did.

A few minutes later, he knocks on the door and the President answers to let him in. Edgar says, "Good evening Mr. President; I am here to assist the First Lady in packing per her request." The President smiles and shakes his hand and invites him in telling Edgar his wife can be found in the closet. Edgar looks at the President and says, "Sir...I came out of it years ago." The President gives Edgar a strange look and then laughs and says, "Oh...I get it...sorry it has been a long day." Edgar excuses himself and heads for the First Lady's closet. The President just stands there scratching his head thinking to himself. "Doesn't this just beat all? My wife and her gay assistant are packing my bags."

The next morning came early as the President's security came to get their bags and escort him and the First Lady to the Marine Corps One Helicopter soon after they had their breakfast.

As they took off for Camp David looking forward for a few days to just unwind.

Chapter 10

The President and First Lady were quiet the whole trip there. Upon arriving, the keeper of the residence was prepared for the two of them as well as the security team and had the kitchen and bar stocked for five days. The President's personal secretary back in Washington was given direct orders not to let anyone know where they were but to go ahead and notify the Camp David staff of the discretionary trip and that they were probably going to stay a few days and to prepare appropriately for their arrival.

The fireplace in the den was crackling as it was raining outside and it kept the house from being so humid. The President and First Lady both got comfortable in their usual chairs as he grabbed a book by the end table and she started flipping through the pages of a fashion magazine. The house staff took their luggage and unpacked for them in the master suite while the security team went to their quarters leaving a front and back guard at the residence who took their positions for the next four hour rotation.

The kitchen staff was busy making a light lunch for the President and the First Lady, while the resident chef was on the internet looking at recipes for the evening meal.

Baking fresh croissants and stuffing them with a lobster salad and served with fried pickles and sweet tea with chocolate chip cookies for desert, was one of the President's favorite.

Putting down the book and smelling the air of baked bread and cookies made him hungry. Looking over at the First Lady, he says to her, "That just smells wonderful doesn't it?" She replies, "Yes and I am getting hungry too. I just love to come here because it feels so much like home." Both the President and the First Lady looked forward to enjoying some quiet time for a few days. They didn't even turn on the television or the radio. Deciding that they would deal with whatever came their way, when they got back from their overseas trip. After all no-one knew that they were even in the Country so they thought it was best to step away from the media for a little while.

Choosing not to eat in the dining room, trays were set up so that they could eat lunch in the den where they were. Afterward the President dozed off in his chair as the First Lady went into their suite to take a quick nap on the soft down mattress.

That afternoon the President and First Lady spent the day playing cards and just enjoying each other's company.

A late supper was planned and the resident chef had fixed them venison medallions with a cherry burgundy sauce, garlic mashed potatoes and fresh sautéed green beans with almond slices and orange sherbet for desert; the chef wanted them to have something of substance since the weather had a chill in the air.

The few days that they were there it rained. Starting to get cabin fever, the First Lady suggested that they go ahead and fly over, stopping in Paris for a day or two and then they could continue onto Istanbul. The President agreed and so the staff packed up their luggage and they left Camp David for the New York Airport where the Air Force One was waiting in a hanger for the President's arrival.

Chapter 11

The trip to Paris was exciting for the First Lady for she had a cousin that had married a Royal and she was looking forward to the drive in the countryside and to see her cousin Lilly's castle and catch up on what was going on in her life.

The limousine picked up the President and First Lady on the tarmac as they got off the plane in Paris and drove them out to the rolling hills of the ancient but beautifully restored country estate. Lilly had mentioned before to her cousin Alex (the First Lady) that the castle which was named the Chateaux de Saint Marten, and had been in her husband's father's family since the 1300's. The large estate filled with sheep and vineyards and various fruit orchards, was a stunning sight to see with the stone wall fence running the perimeter of the property. Lilly had also mentioned that the stone wall fence was actually older than the castle itself. However, it was the gardens that just took the President's breath away. The flowers were of old seeds that you don't see any more that had been harvested every year and replanted. Both he and the First Lady were taken by the care that the heirs had for their ancestral lands.

Lilly's husband Andre' invited the President into his library for a bottle of wine from his private stock. Over two hundred years old; La Tache was not only the name of the wine, but also the name of the vineyard that had been in the Ronanai family for generations; which was on his mother's side and in another town of France that his sister had inherited. The President was looking forward to being entertained by this French Nobleman with all his stories of the family history. After all the President just loved history, it was his favorite subject when he was in school.

This was a great side trip for both the First Lady and the President as they had a lovely visit and could be themselves, away from the responsibility of being a head of state. The next afternoon they left and drove back into Paris and then headed off for Istanbul.

Chapter 12

Upon arriving at the airport, a red carpet was placed at the bottom of the steps of the Air Force One as they President and First Lady got off the plane. The news reporters had been hanging out at the airport for two days wondering what had happened to them, for they were expected to arrive the day before.

Greeted by the Prime Minister himself, they were escorted to their hotel and the concierge' handed the President an itinerary of what the Prime Minister had planned for their time together in Turkey. He also handed the First Lady an itinerary as well as told her that the Prime Minister had made arrangements for his wife to accompany her when she was not with her husband and that there was plenty of activities planned for the two of them.

An early dinner was scheduled for that afternoon and it was a formal affair full of dignitaries; and that a limousine would be awaiting them at their hotel at three o'clock to take them to the Prime Minister's Estate.

As the bellman escorted them to the penthouse suite and was showing them the oversized suite and where everything was; a member of the hotel staff knocked on the door to assist the

First Lady in unpacking her and the President's things as well as to see if she needed anything.

With pen and labels in hand she told the First Lady that she would go ahead and label all the drawers for her and the President's convenience and that she would take care of everything and didn't need any assistance unless the First Lady just wanted to sit and chat while she was unpacking. When the First Lady replied in a Turkish dialect, the woman unpacking their things went back to speaking her native tongue and the two women just chatted away like best of friends. The First Lady thought it would be good for her to brush up on her Turkish language that she very rarely ever spoke except on special occasions, so this was a real treat. Knowing that she was going to spend time with the Prime Minister's wife, it would do her well to practice a little before the afternoon event. The First Lady was actually quite a linguist for she spoke several languages. This was a real bonus for the President when he would go overseas for his wife could translate for him. She spoke Spanish, Italian, Greek, French, Russian, German and the Turkish language. She never could quite get the Asian languages though. Fortunately most upper class Middle Eastern people speak French, so she never bothered with Arabic.

When the packing was done, the First Lady called down for room service and ordered a light snack knowing full well that the afternoon meal would probably be quite a spread; but she and the President were a little hungry so they had a snack of fruit and cheeses sent up.

Taking the time to unwind after the plane trip the President takes the deck of cards out of his pocket and plays a game of solitaire while the First Lady wanders around the suite checking everything out and laying the President's clothes out for the social event that afternoon. Going back into her closet, she looks through her things as she picks out just the right outfit for the afternoon so as to blend in with the culture, so not to be offensive. She wanted to be sure that the Prime Minister's wife would feel comfortable with her and by showing respect by her clothing it would be more appropriate. After all she was a woman in a male dominated country and it was better all-around to be respectful of their ways. Time passed quickly as the President looked at his watch and says to the First Lady, "We need to get ready, for our chariot awaits downstairs dear," as he hands her one of her shoes. The First Lady reaches over and puts her hand on the side of his face and says to him. "I just love your sense of humor that is why I married you dear." They both giggle as they quickly get ready and head down the elevator to the limousine waiting for them at the front door.

As they arrived at the Prime Ministers estate which was overwhelmed by dignitaries from all over the world; the chauffer opened the door for the President and First Lady to get out as they were greeted by the Prime Minister and his wife. For the first half hour both the men and women mingled about the main entrance gallery with introductions, then they retreated to the two separate dining areas, one for the men in the east wing dining hall and the women went into the west dining room hall which was made of glass and overlooked the gardens; standard tables and chairs were set up with formal china and silverware and a lighter fare was served.

As the men all settled into their Turkish pillows, the music started and the belly dancers entertained them as lamb and vegetables with mint tea was served on the small tables between all of the pillows. Since there were strict Muslims at this event, alcohol was not served at the meal as to show respect for their beliefs. As the President says to the Prime Minister beside him, "I was just joking to my wife about the belly dancers, this is great. Thank you so much for the hospitality." The Prime Minister replies, "It is part of the culture; outsiders really do enjoy it though, especially Americans." As the afternoon goes on and the meal is finished, the men divide off; some go back into the gallery to talk among themselves, while others go to the smoking room for a cigar and those who drink a brandy.

The President and the Prime Minister step away from the crowded room as the two of them finally have a chance to have some one on one conversation. The gardens at the estate are stunning and this puts the President at ease. The Prime Minister is aware of the Garbage Barge Bill and he knows that this President is dying to talk about it so he discretely brings it up. "President Kent, what does your Country do about

Waste-Pickers?" He says. The President looks at him a little odd and replies, "I've never heard that term used before, what is a waste-picker?" The Prime Minister snickers a moment then says, "People who live on other people's garbage by recycling the metal, glass, paper, plastic, and such." The President replies, "I've never heard of that? How funny! You mean that people actually go Dumpster Diving?" The Prime Minister starts to laugh and says, "I have never heard it called that, you've got one on me." They both start to chuckle. The President then says, "We sure could use some of that at home, because we have a real problem with an abundance of waste and no place to put it."

The Prime Minister sits at a small table in the middle of the garden as a waiter comes out with a tray of tea and sets the cups on saucers on the table then pours the tea into each of the cups leaving the teapot on the table and then quickly disappears. The Prime Minister asks the President to join him. Then the Prime Minister says to the President, "The waste pickers here are actually a benefit to the economy because they are saving millions of materials that would otherwise have to be disposed of. This would cause hardship for we do not have an abundance of land to waste. Also by recycling we close that loop.

Believe it or not we have a quarter of a million waste pickers here in Turkey, of which over 100,000 are here in the city of Istanbul." The President gasps, "You are kidding?" The Prime Minister replies, "No, I am serious, it is big business. Most of the garbage pickers are men that live close by upper class neighborhoods and they freelance, so they are actually off the record workers. I believe in your country you refer them as under the radar or off the grid." The President nods his head and says, "I know what you mean. They don't pay taxes." The Prime Minister shaking his head, "Yes, however we are looking into this situation but we have found that these independents insist on freelancing due to the flexibility they have and the income can be substantial rather than working an hourly job at an hourly wage. It appears it is in their best interest to be independent. I personally understand this from their point of view; however territorial disputes usually end up with violent results. Then there is other problems with disease and such, you know health issues. So we have our own problems here as well; although they are not as expansive as what I read about in the American papers." He pauses for a moment then says, "I have to tell you I find that word Dumpster Diving quite humorous." As the Prime Minister starts to laugh again. The President smiling says, "Yes that is what we call it back home, however it is not the same and ironically Waste-Picking has not caught on in America; although I do like the recycling bit. I think that is where the future needs to be. By recycling we protect the environment as well as we become more aware of the products we buy as well as use. It is definitely a mindset that needs to be taught in the lower grade schools so that the children grow up aware. It is hard to teach the older generation that are set in their ways." The Prime Minister says to the President, "You have to set mandatory recycling laws, otherwise it won't work. Sometimes you just have to just say NO. It may not be popular, but then a lot of times doing what is best for all is not popular. At the end of the day doing what is right is what you take home." The President looks at the Prime Minister and says, "You are a wise man. I respect what you say. It is important at the end of the day, not only that, you sleep better at night knowing you stood your ground." The Prime Minister replies, "Exactly." He pauses for a moment then says, "So what are you planning to do about your trash problem?" The President replies, "Borrow your Trash-Pickers?" Both of the men start laughing; then the President says, "Recycling is definitely a major part of the plan. We however have such an abundance of garbage; we are going to have to use incinerators until we get this under control. Then there is the whole toxic waste issues that have to be addressed. Right now I am looking into the cost of this ordeal to get creative financing and try to get rid of some of this debt too." The Prime Minister says, "I saw your speech on the television a few nights ago. I think that is a very good move that you are making. We don't have those resources here. Military patents, now that is very interesting and I have to commend you; that is a smart business move. If you do a 50/50 deal, that is a lot of income you are bringing into the economy as well as the budget if you can keep control of Congress not spending it as fast as it comes in." The President nodding his head states, "I will have to address that when I get back. I can see Washington now; I bet every Lobbyist in town is foaming at the mouth." The Prime Minister smiles and says, "Yes, I bet they are. That kind of money, the thieves are preparing for their attack, shall I loan you my magic carpet?" Suddenly smiling he just nods his head in agreement and says, "Yes, nice thought... however, I don't think running away is the answer; I am not looking forward to having to reel in Congress at all. I am going to have to nip this one in the bud from the get go. This money needs to be apportioned for the necessary incinerators and the rest needs to go to paying down the debt, and only the debt until it is paid off. I know that this is going to be a real battle, because they will find ways to manipulate it. But I am going to head it off with an Executive Order. It is the only way I know how to deal with this." The Prime Minister says, "That is what I mean by standing your ground, and I respect you as well. I have to tell you this parlay has been admirable. Shall we return to the house? I am sure they are wondering what we are up to," as the President and the Prime Minister both get up and walk back to the mansion.

Chapter 13

Meanwhile back in Washington. The chaos is building. The Lobbyists are calling and the phones are all ringing off the hook. The tavern where everyone hangs out is filled with Congressman, Senators, and various staff members all gossiping with rumors. High ranking Officers are being jetted off to Caribbean Islands on vacations as the big businessmen are wining and dining them to gain favor. It is business as usual in the town while the cat is away.

The stock market is creeping up with the plans of expansion that the rumors of money bring. Under the table deals are being made by the Representatives and the Corporate Officers.   Everyone is looking to have their hands filled working some kind of deal. Preliminary Bills are being drafted to divert the money to special interest groups. Everyone in Washington is planning on getting their hands on this new found treasure.

At the White House the staff is busy as well.   The phones are ringing and everyone wants to know how the President is going to distribute the patents and when. While Senator Gene Baker's office is just as busy as well with businessmen trying to get an appointment with the executor of this

Bill to find out any information they can.

Senator Baker decided to also take a trip out of the Country to avoid what he expected would happen when the President left. The staff in his office was being bombarded by every businessman in the Country. Gift baskets were everywhere; so many that the staff had to take them to a warehouse and the ones with food were given to the local food bank. It was obvious what was going on. Everyone was trying to jump on this bandwagon of opportunity.

Back in Turkey...The First Lady spent the next day shopping with her entourage and having a wonderful time with the Prime Minister's wife, whom suggested that they take a day to visit the Museum of Creation; a place that few American's actually know about or even go to.

They have a wonderful lunch at a little café' and the whole experience is quite a refreshing change. "It is so nice to just enjoy a day without politics," the First Lady thinks to herself and speaking the language with all the women in the group was fun too. It was a great girl's day out.

A few days later as they are winding down the trip, and thanking everyone for all of their hospitality, the President and the First Lady were excited about their next stop.

Upon arrival in Amman, Jordan; the President and the First Lady again were chauffeured to their hotel the day before the party as to have time to get situated before the big event.

The First Lady arranges an intimate dinner for her and her husband on the large patio overlooking the city that evening for they have been so busy she felt that they needed some romantic time alone.

Unlike most Presidential families, they never had any children and spent all their time together supporting each other's careers. At this point in their lives they accepted the fact that there would be no children and it was alright. There were plenty of nephews and nieces to spoil.

The President and First Lady had a wonderful evening together and the morning came quickly.

A knock on the door and it was breakfast being served again on the outside patio. The thick coffee was strong and the pastries were fresh with a large bowl of fresh cut up fruit and the latest copy of The New York Times; which the President grabbed up quickly to see what was in it. The First Lady walks out on the deck and bends over to kiss her husband then sits across from him as she starts to sip on her coffee. Both sitting in their robes they felt right at home.

The First Lady looks at her husband and says, "Anything interesting in that paper?" The President looks up over the newsprint and says, "Same old thing, different day." Putting down the paper he starts to eat his breakfast as they chat about nothing.

Chapter 14

It was several hours before they were to meet with the King so the President and the First Lady had some time to get ready before being escorted to the King's Palace.

The First Lady has the hotel take the wrinkles out of her new outfit that her friend had given to her to wear and went through several scarves to find just the right one. She also had the staff steam the President's suit and iron his shirt.

Before long they were at the Palace in all its grandeur. As they went their separate ways, he with the King and the

First Lady went into the hen parlor to be with the women, which she was aware that it was just the culture and how things were done over there. She actually liked the fact that she could laugh and giggle with the women and talk about everything but politics. It was refreshing to her.

The President being introduced to the new King was surprised at how well read this young King was.

When they got away from the crowd and had a chance to talk one on one; the King of Jordan says to the President, "Over the past few years we have grown at a faster pace than ever before. The economy has picked up substantially and the automobile is now a common household item whereas ten years ago this was not the case here in Amman. Life has definitely changed here in the city. We had a transit system that worked well before the automobile. However with the demand for private vehicles here in the city, we now are going to have to reconfigure the amount of traffic and the amount of garbage because they both are vying for space and have both gone beyond capacity."

The President raises his eyebrows and says to the King, "I was not aware of this. Please go on I am very interested in what you have to say." The King continues, "In the past, public transportation was an integral part of the cities movement; however now with the automobile growing in rapid numbers; our streets once full of pedestrians walking the street lined markets, have recently become highways for the large numbers of privately owned vehicles. Because of this, the trash pickup that went from individual properties, both residential and commercial, we had to set up dumpsters on every street as a community container. This worked out fine in the beginning; now it has become a disaster and a real health issue since development has filled all the vacant lots and the containers are now on the streets in front of people's houses and obviously this causes problems between neighbors." The President nods his head and says, "Oh... I can understand how I would feel if there was a dumpster with trash in front of my home." The King replies, "Exactly... This situation has escalated to a point that something has to drastically change. Many of the residences are now utilizing the original bins that were set up before the community dumpsters were put in and the waste management pickup vehicles are servicing these families on a regular basis. The cost of this is added to the electric bills since we have had to expand the manpower, trucks, fuel, and maintenance in order to keep up with the ever growing population." Again the President nods and says, "You really do have some serious issues in this area as well." The King with a stern look on his face says, "Yes we do and we are taking this matter to heart. We are now looking into recycling and asking the public to do their part in separating their trash. One for metal, one for plastic, one for paper, and so forth and so on. By recycling, we should reduce waste considerably. Paper and cardboard alone is one third of the waste. Ironically in some of the Middle-Eastern cities they actually feed the camels cardboard due to the fact there is little grass for them to eat. I have personally seen this. It is amazing and funny when you think about it, whereas paper and cardboard can actually be a resource, which could generate income and create jobs; instead of being a burden, a health issue or an environmental liability. Our studies have shown that we generate less than half of what is produced in the United States, which has the highest waste in the world. As a middle income country, we can't handle what waste we have." The President says to the King, "I see that you have delved heavily into this situation. I have the same concerns except our problems are on a much larger scale. This problem I am sure is worldwide, as we become more and more of a global community. I am very curious of how all the countries around the globe are handling these problems. I understand that we are on the top of the pile when it comes to this abundance of waste issue. It is an embarrassment to the world that we as a Country have allowed ourselves to get into this predicament." The King pauses for a moment then says to the President, "Actually I spent some time recently in your Country as I was invited to visit friends on the Island of Nantucket, off the coast of Massachusetts. Much to my surprise, I found that this tiny community really has it together and was quite impressed as to the extent that they controlled their waste. This affluent island village surrounded by water, has no place for landfills, due to the high property values, it is not financially feasible. The town council I was told instituted strict recycling policies sending the separated items to various recycling center to be handled. I was told that food waste is composted and returned to the soil and that the used oil from the restaurants was sold to a refiner to be used for ethanol. This apparently only leaves eight (8) percent that has to be shipped off the island to a landfill. What I found most interesting is the fact that in other cities in Massachusetts they are sending sixty-six (66) percent of waste to the landfills; which is a big division between the two." The President is amazed at these statistics and says to him. I am ashamed to admit it, but I had no idea that Nantucket was so pro-active. When I get back home, I will definitely look into their program. This is something that we need to expand on throughout our Country. I greatly appreciate you telling me this. I am also going to find out why I was never told about this. Again I respect your knowledge of what is going on in my own backyard." The President was embarrassed that this information had been held from him and he made a mental note to address this when he gets back from his trip.

The King again starts speaking, "What I am most concerned with is the waste management even more than I am of the increasing traffic issues, because a working mass transit system, which we did have several years ago, can be put back into place as we had originally, this will resolve itself in time. The problem which can be easily fixed is due to neglect due to the ever growing population investing in private vehicles. We are currently looking into restructuring our Countries infrastructure to handle a modern mass transit system."

At that point the President asks, "I am interested in seeing what your plans are for this. I have been to Greece and they have an excellent mass transit system that appears to work well." The

King smiles and says, "Yes, I too have been there and we are actually working with the designers of that system and molding it to accommodate our needs and resolve the lack of proper highways which we have a shortage of. Being what you would consider a biblical country; we are an old civilization that was built way before anyone even imagined an automobile."

The President then replies, "You have a very good point there. We in the United States are a new Country and it is easy for us to create infrastructure since we do not have thousands of years of history buried under cities as you do. I can see the concerns and historic responsibility and the values of what is under the sand here in your Country. I agree that this is a major issue when dealing with infrastructure since you never know what will be found. When you think about it, the trash that they buried all those centuries ago tells us about how they lived, which is fortuitous."

The King then replies, "Yes it is and to resolve our solid waste issues we need to get rid of the community dumpsters and go back to our old system of individual property pickup for both residences and businesses. I feel that this will bring an improvement to cleaning up our streets. After all recycling will also greatly reduce the amount of garbage that has to be dealt with and will also reduce environmental impacts as well as reduce pressure on the few landfills we have. I am also looking at turning this over the private sector, for they have proven to be more suitable to handle all of this as well as to make it profitable; whereas the governing entity can focus on other problems."

The President at that point says, "The private sector in America financially as done well overseeing the Waste Management, however due to the large amount of garbage in the cities, it is tough to get a handle on this problem, especially with accountability on their end for actually doing what needs to be done. We need tougher recycling laws and we need to change the attitudes such as you spoke of in Nantucket. I am sure by your knowledge that you already have a handle on what the rules will be when you turn this over to the private sector as far as their accountability. This is something that we as Americans need to respect; the accountability for our actions. I really do appreciate all that we have talked about and you have given me a lot to think about as well to address when I get back to Washington as I greatly appreciate your wisdom."

The King ends the conversation with this, "The number one issue is that it is the civic responsibility of each individual to be responsible for the health of their communities as well as the city itself. So we as rulers are really relying on each individual to do their part in assisting Amman with our waste issues by being accountable for their own actions."

As the King and the President walk back into the gallery of dignitaries and blend into the crowd.

Chapter 15

On the other side of the mansion the women are giggling and having a wonderful time sharing stories of family and children. When the First Lady tells the women that she was not able to have children; their faces showed sadness, however the First Lady told them it was fine she had lots of nieces and nephews that she could spoil and send back home, and they all laughed. The evening turned out very informative for the President and the First Lady rather enjoyed her evening with the ladies of Jordan.

As the night got late, the President had a waiter send for his wife in the other room and let her know that it was soon time to go and that the women could now join their husbands. As they all stepped out to the gallery to join the men.

Saying their goodbyes and thanking the King and his wife for their hospitality they exited the room and walked out of the mansion where the private limousine was waiting to take the President back to his hotel escorted by his security team that had waited outside that evening.

Upon reaching their hotel the First Lady asked the President how his evening went. He replies, "I have to tell you that I was actually a little embarrassed that the King knew more about what was going on in Nantucket than I did." The First Lady responds quickly, "What are you talking about?" The President says, "Do you know that Nantucket already has a plan in action and that only 8 percent of the trash on that island goes to a landfill?" The First Lady looks surprised and says, "No, I did not know that and why were we not told of this?" The President replies, "Obviously someone is not doing their job of keeping me informed. I will get to the bottom of this when we get back. I want to know what every town is doing; and why is it that only Nantucket has got it together? What is wrong with the rest of the State of Massachusetts?" The First Lady replies, "That is a good questions, you need to have an audience with the Governor, Congressman and Senator of Massachusetts and ask them that question?

May I also suggest that the staff get a copy of this so that it is on your desk when we get back, what do you think?"

The President replies, "Yes, that is exactly what I need to do right away." As he dials his cell phone to Washington to let Johnathon know of his request; as well as telling him to let the staff know of the embarrassing situation he was in by not having any information on the Nantucket project.

Johnathon apologizes to the President and says that none of the staff had ever been to Nantucket and that he would get right on it as well as have the staff investigate if there were any other small affluent towns that also had a handle on the waste problems that they did not know about; and that he would have all the information that they could find out on his desk when he arrived back home in Washington in a few days.

Upon arriving back at their hotel, the First Lady stopped at the front desk and asked that they bring up some coffee and sandwiches up to the room as well as something sweet for desert; and that the President was hungry for a light snack and it had been a long evening.

The desk clerk replied that he would have it delivered right away; as the President and First Lady got on the elevator and went up to their suite for the evening as the security guards stood watch at the outside door.

Within twenty minutes there was a knock on the door as the hotel waiter brought in their snack on a rolling tray. The First Lady tipped the waiter and told him thank you and that would be all.

In some ways the two of them were looking forward to coming home even though there was so much work to do and so much research to check out to be sure that the President had all the facts. It had been an informative trip even with the embarrassing conversation with the King of Jordan. All in all it was what the President needed to get the country back on track with cleaning up the landfills and getting a handle on all of this.

Chapter 16

The next morning the President told his security that he and the First Lady were staying in for the day and to cancel their day trip into town. They were both exhausted and just needed some time to rest before the long trip home to Washington.

Ordering in breakfast the two of them ate on the outside patio as they enjoyed the view from the balcony just watching everyone below hurry about. It was a quiet morning and relaxing not to have to have meetings or deal with the usual nonsense that comes with the job. Both the President and the First Lady sat and read the paper while they drank their coffee. Afterward the President made his way over to the couch and picked up a book that he had started to read and never found the time to finish it. While the First Lady got out her Kindle to download another mystery novel from her favorite author and settled into the chair across from the President. Within fifteen minutes the President had dozed off on the couch as the First Lady went into their bedroom to get a light blanket and covered up her husband, then went back to reading her story. Every so often she would look over at him and smile seeing him resting. She knew how stressful this life was and she could see the gray in his hair was getting thicker.

Although she was completely supportive of what he was doing, she was looking forward to the end of this term and going back to having a normal life. It was an exciting adventure though she had to admit.

Several hours later the President awoke feeling rested and asked the First Lady how she felt about playing a game of cards. She had just finished her book and turned her Kindle off; as she walked over to the table to shuffle the deck of cards. This was actually something that they had done all of their married life. Playing a game of cards was a stable factor in their life. It didn't matter what they did or where life took them; the cards went too. So they spent the rest of the afternoon just playing cards.

It was around four o'clock and the First Lady called down to order dinner since they hadn't had anything since breakfast. She also asked if the concierge could send someone up to help pack since they were leaving in the morning. The concierge said he would send up one of the housekeepers after they finished their meal as not to disturb them while they ate. Later that evening the housekeeper came up and helped the First Lady pack up their bags for their trip back to Washington.

Morning came quickly and the President and his wife left for the airport heading back to the states. The trip was long and both the President and First Lady did their best to just rest the whole flight home. Not much was said between the two of them.

Before long they were back in Washington and the hustle and bustle of life on the hill. Jonathon had scheduled a meeting with the gentlemen that were representing the State of Massachusetts first thing the next morning as they sat outside of the Oval Office awaiting the President.

Brantley was also next in line to see the President with the list of items that could be cut from the budget.

Senator Gene Baker and Senator Tom Edwards were also waiting to also see the President.

As the President comes into the office through the back door and makes himself comfortable before the meeting as he rings Shelly to bring some coffee for himself and his guests and to go ahead and show them in.

As the Governor, Congressman and Senator of Massachusetts take a seat, the President asks them if they would like some coffee as Shelly brings in a tray and serves the gentleman.

Upon her leaving she closes the door behind her knowing what was coming up next.

The President was unusually calm though... as he says to them, "Gentleman, what in the hell is going on in your State that Nantucket has a handle on the garbage situation and the rest of the State is an absolute mess. Also why was I not told about the successes of Nantucket?

I have to tell you I was absolutely embarrassed that the King of Jordan knew more of what was going on in our country than I was. This is unacceptable. What do you plan on doing about this?"

The Governor speaks up, "Mr. President, we were not aware that you did not know what was going on in this little town. Because it is an exclusive resort area with a small population and adequate financial resources as well as the cooperation of its residents; the strict recycling laws work. Everyone does their part to keep their town clean. Unfortunately this does not work in the big cities. We have too many social problems with the poor and homeless as well as the gangs that only add to the problem. We have implemented recycling in the schools as well as the residential areas and are trying to get the local residences to separate their trash in bins that we supply. Some people cooperate and some don't care. Ironically we have found that the upper classes are supportive of our efforts while in the poor neighborhoods we are just wasting our time and money because they don't use the bins and frankly don't care."

The President stands up and replies, "So it is a class thing? Well that it interesting? I found that in Turkey the poor collect the garbage and actually make an income from recycling. Whereas here in America the poor just don't give a damn, is that what you are telling me?" The Governor replies, "Yes sir, that seems to be the problem and we really don't know what to do about people being lazy."

The President replies, "Well apparently you need to cut them off of social programs or at least make them work for a check." The Governor says, "You mean like the CCC back in the Depression?" The President replies, "Yes, that is exactly what I am saying. Create jobs of picking up trash if you have to. Give them a broom and a trash bag and send them on the streets to clean them up like the prison labor does on the highway. It is time for a hand up not a hand out. These welfare checks are doing nothing to help people help themselves. Make them work for it. They can pick up cigarette butts. They can pick up trash. They can plant flowers and trees and make their areas nice. People need to have pride in where they live. They need to feel useful otherwise they become slothful and that is what welfare has done. We need to change this. Because it is obvious by the actions of the people that welfare does not work and it has become abused. When something is taken for granted it is time to change it. So what I suggest is workfare not welfare; and we will use your State as the trial run for the whole country. Matter of fact, I was in Jamaica and they actually pay people to sweep the sidewalks for their welfare check. If they can do it there than why aren't we doing it here? I expect you to have this implemented right away and I want to see the results in six months. Ok gentlemen this meeting is over. You have your work cut out for you. Thank you for your valuable time." As the President escorts the men to the door and Brantley sits outside waiting his turn.

The President looks at Brantley and tells him to give him ten minutes then to come on in as he walks back to his desk to write down some notes on a legal pad he keeps of the day's activities.

A little while later Brantley comes into the office with a hand full of files as he goes to the large table at the east end of the office. "Mr. President," as Brantley addresses him. "I had my team go over some cuts that we can make which we will do gradually but it will make a big impact on creating the funds for the incinerators. I also have the list of items that General Canton gave me on the military side of patents that can be of benefit to the open market and have been approved by Homeland Security as safe to release into the marketplace. The income of a joint venture with private industry should cut the military budget substantially coming from the taxpayers; therefore utilizing the income from the royalties to finance the military itself. As a result, we can actually make a dent in balancing the budget as well as have the funding for the incinerator program." As the President sits down beside Brantley and they go over the list while the President writes down everything on his legal pad. The two of them spend several hours going over the list of programs to be eliminated upon completion of the period of the grants that have been issued as to let those know who are receiving them that once the time period is over, that there will not be another approval for those funds and that those individuals will have to look elsewhere at private industry for funding.

Once that is finalized Brantley and the President again review the list of all the patented items that the military has stuffed in a drawer that can be used for non-military resources that is useful and safe to society as well as the environment.

Looking at his watch he picks up the phone and has Shelly bring in some lunch for himself and the Senators who were patiently waiting as he excuses Brantley.

Chapter 17

Senators Baker and Edwards enter the office shaking hands with the President asking him about his trip as they shared small talk for about fifteen minutes when Shelly knocks on the door then brings in a large tray with various sandwiches and salads and sets it on the small conference table on the east side of the room. Johnathon is behind her with a pot of coffee and cups as well as a pitcher of tea and a plate of cookies. The two of them set up the table then leave quickly closing the door behind them.

The President says, "Shall we have a bite to eat gentlemen?" Both of the Senators nod their heads and walk over to the conference table and pull up chairs as the three of them fix their plates and sit down for lunch and conversation. The President proceeds to say, "I had a very embarrassing situation in Jordan on my trip with the King. Apparently he was more informed of the situation in Nantucket than I was." Senator Baker replies, "Sir, I don't follow you?" The President says, "Well Nantucket has a real handle on their waste situation. Only eight percent of the waste actually goes to a landfill. They have mandatory recycling laws and everyone on the island works together to keep their island clean. I had a meeting just this morning with the gentlemen in power in Massachusetts and told them they are basically the Ginny-pig for a clean-up program. I wanted to let you both in on what I told them was going to happen. Much like the CCC back in the great depression; welfare will be a workfare test program. Jobs will be found even if it is sweeping the sidewalks or shoveling snow in the winter. They have been given six months to implement a successful working program that will put the pride back in the people and make them feel useful again." Senator Edwards smiling says, "Sir that is a great idea. We need to implement that all over the country. When you think about it we are paying them anyway, why not get something out of it. Older people on fixed incomes who are not able to mow their yards or fix their roof or paint their homes will have the opportunity to have repairs done that otherwise could not afford it. This is a good thing. This is bringing the country together as a family. Like the old barn raising back in the days of my grandfather. If you don't mind I would like to talk with the governor of Kentucky about this. I think that it would go over well in my State; especially it being one of the Southern States. We could really push the southern hospitality button on this issue." Senator Baker speaks, "Well let me tell you New Jersey is going to have the same issues as all of the big cities. I am not looking forward to it either. With the large separation of classes it will be a tough battle. I will be interested in seeing what Massachusetts will bring to the table and maybe we can follow their lead." The President says, "It is time we run this country like a business. If I ran a business like what we have done over the years with our finances, I would have filed bankruptcy years ago. This is not what our forefathers intended. We need to get a handle on this situation before it goes too far." Both of the Senators agree with the President.

"Now as far as the incinerator program", the President says, "I had a meeting with Brantley and he gave me a list of the Grants that we will be not renewing when their time expires." Both Senators get real quiet knowing that their constituents will be angry about this move.

The President speaks up again, "The good news is that I also have here a list of patents that can be marketed and used in the public sector that are both safe and environmentally friendly. I propose that we put these items out for bid as a joint venture with our fifty percent going to the military budget and the money that was used for the military will be forwarded to the purchase of incinerators and programs for recycling and cleaning up landfills. I believe this is called the old bait and switch. However we are not using that term. What we are showing the public is that we are creating a self-supporting military that is not a burden to the taxpayers. I believe that this will work." Senator Baker nods his head and says, "Sir that is absolutely incredible. It will work. The American People will love it. What you are showing by your actions is accountability... Sir that is what we need. Yes, this is a doable situation. Creates jobs, cuts taxes; yes the people will love it. The businesses will love it. This is a win-win situation."

The President just smiles for a moment not saying anything.

Senator Edwards then replies, "Sir, how are you going to put these products out there for bid?" The President replies, "Same way we do with military contracts; however all bids will be with American Contractors and all products are to be made here in America. This will go with the cleaning up of our country as well, especially with the downgrading of grants and our new workfare programs that we will be implementing. I think that we can actually merge all of this together to successfully pull this off. I have given this a lot of thought and by pulling from different resources we are giving the

American people opportunities to get back on their feet with paying jobs that give them pride in what they are doing as well as gets them off their asses." Both of the Senators laugh at the President's remark. Senator Baker then states, "Sir the American people are going to love this. We need these programs implemented immediately. I know there will be a little grumbling from overseas companies; however you are doing what is best for our country. We need to take care of our own backyard first. By taking this initiative and showing that we are taking the lead in cleaning up our environment, reducing our spending in Washington and being accountable is top notch in my book. We are taking the bull by the horns and getting our act together and this shows integrity Sir. It shows the world we as a country have integrity by our actions."

The President says to his comrades, "When I was in Istanbul last week I was very impressed by the fact that some people actually live on other people's garbage by recycling. I was taken by the entrepreneurial spirit that these people had. I had jokingly mentioned to the Prime Minister of Turkey, that I would like to borrow what they call the Waste-Pickers. He and I laughed about it, but I was serious at the time. This trip for me was very enlightening to see how other countries deal with their own problems. I think that in the future our relationships with other countries need to be based on finding a common ground with problems that affect our environment rather than fighting over our cultural differences; for we all have the same problems and we can learn from one another how to handle situations as well as respect the fact that we all are different and have the right to be different. We don't have to be the same, just respect others space and beliefs as you would want to have them do."

Senator Edwards says, "Well Sir, we have our hands full with all of this. You may want to let Congress in on your plans and it looks like a whole new ballgame for Washington."

The President says to Senator Baker, "What ever happened to that Garbage Barge anyway?"

Senator Baker replies, "Sir I heard some company up north had offered to purchase what was left of the garbage still on the barge that had not been lost in the ocean due to storms. I was told that they will recycle what they can and they have incinerators to handle all the contaminable and toxic waste."

The President says, "I'm glad to see that someone saw that we had a problem and had the integrity to step up to the plate and to do what is right."

The End

Research for this book came from:

- (The local people I spoke with while visiting Turkey.)
- Urban Crossroads
- The Waste Pickers of Istanbul
- US Congress – Open Congress (Internet)
- And of course...special thanks to my Mother's vast knowledge of Washington.

About the Author

As in all her books, Darla Mae Dudley combines facts with fiction, to bring the reader's into her stories as they go back and personally ask themselves "where was I, when all these things happened." She calls it "NONFICTION-FANTASY" as she dresses up reality. Having traveled to over 25 countries, she puts her personal experiences into everything she writes and does extensive research on the events that she brings back to life in her stories.

Darla Mae Dudley, Author

Books by this Author:

A Dying Breed

Flatwoods,

As Revelations Told

Fulfillment of a Fantasy

Earth's Blood

Under My Roof Under My Rules

Memoirs of a Southern Woman

Colors of Appalachia (picture)

A Day at the Beach (picture)

Little Mountain Warriors

Coming Soon:

- Women Protect Your Assets
- Looking out the Window at Changes of Life (Romance – This is a Sequel)

www.ingramcontent.com/pod-product-compliance
Lightning Source LLC
Chambersburg PA
CBHW060455290526
45791CB00001B/122